The Politics of Size

The Politics of Size

REPRESENTATION IN THE
UNITED STATES, 1776–1850

Rosemarie Zagarri

Cornell University Press

Ithaca and London

First published 1987 by Cornell University Press.

Maps 1, 2, and 3 are adapted by permission of the Carnegie Institute of Washington from Charles O. Paullin, *Atlas of the Historical Geography of the United States*, Publication No. 401 (Baltimore, 1932).

Maps 5 and 6 are reprinted from Lester J. Cappon et al., eds., *Atlas of Early American History: The Revolutionary Era, 1760–1790*, pp. 25 and 62. Copyright © 1976 by Princeton University Press; published for the Newberry Library and the Institute of Early American History and Culture by Princeton University Press. The two maps are reprinted with permission of Princeton University Press.

International Standard Book Number 0-8014-2019-9
Library of Congress Catalog Card Number 87-47609
Printed in the United States of America
Librarians: Library of Congress cataloging information appears on the last page of the book.

The paper in this book is acid-free and meets the guidelines for permanence and durability of the Committee on Production Guidelines for Book Longevity of the Council on Library Resources.

To Mom, Dad,

Paul, Jolene, Mary Ann, Kathleen, and Linda

Contents

Maps

Contents

Maps

Preface

Historians have long portrayed the conflict between large and small states at the federal Constitutional Convention as something of an anomaly. That conflict, they say, first emerged in Philadelphia during the debate over representation in Congress and ended there with the Great Compromise, giving small states equal representation in the upper house and the large states proportional representation in the lower house. Historians describe the split as transitory, based on expediency, and insignificant in relation to the more important division between North and South. Whatever the short-term bitterness, the controversy, it is said, had no long-term resonance.

Yet such an analysis fails to grasp the depth, complexity, and persistence of the conflict. When the Convention debates are read in the context of other political controversies—in particular, conflicts over representation at both the state and national levels—an impressive and intriguing continuity becomes apparent. State size constituted a basis of division well before and long after the federal Convention. The cleavage can be found in such disparate forums as the debates over removal of state capitals, the reapportionment of state legislatures, the election of congressmen and presidential electors, and the decennial reapportionment of Congress.

In the period 1776–1850, it became clear that states of different sizes actually had distinct approaches to representation. The small states advocated a traditional approach, in which geography defined representative institutions; the large states supported a more innovative view, in which population constituted the most important variable. Not until the mid-nineteenth century did the large states' demographic model completely supersede the small states' approach—with important consequences for the future of congressional politics.

I am pleased to thank all those who have been instrumental in this project. Edmund S. Morgan guided the study through its earliest stages and provided innumerable insights and suggestions for improvement. His patience, his openness to new ideas, and, most of all, his example as a historian made this work possible. Timothy H. Breen first showed me the possibilities for the study of early American history in an undergraduate seminar and has been a loyal supporter ever since. Robert Blobaum, Patricia Cline Cohen, William Cronon, Douglas Greenberg, Drew McCoy, Pauline Maier, Eben Moglen, and J. R. Pole all offered valuable criticisms on earlier versions of the manuscript, and I am grateful to them for their time and effort. I especially thank Peter S. Onuf, who read several drafts and provided thoughtful, detailed, and penetrating commentary. His willingness to engage in an ongoing critical dialogue helped make this a better book. Finally, my husband, Jefferson Morley, believed in the project from the beginning, pushed me to see the implications of my ideas, and exercised his considerable editorial skills on the various versions of each chapter. I could not have completed the book without him.

ROSEMARIE ZAGARRI

Washington, D.C.

The Politics of Size

The Dimensions of
the Problem

The deepest and most antagonistic conflict at the federal Constitutional Convention was the controversy over representation in the national legislature—a conflict that pitted the large states against the small. In the course of debate, it became clear that each side was willing to go to the brink of disunion for its position, nearly bringing the Convention to a premature conclusion. "The disparity of the States in point of size," said one delegate, "was the main difficulty" preventing resolution of the representation question.[1] "Distance," declared Alexander Hamilton, "has a physical effect upon men's minds—."[2]

As historians have usually explained it, the split between large and small states arose from nowhere and disappeared immediately after the Convention. The large- and small-state coalitions, they argue, were alliances based on expediency; the clash, a matter of power rather than of conflicting principles. At most, it masked the more fundamental division between North and South.[3] As plausible as these views may seem,

[1]Max Farrand, ed., *The Records of the Federal Convention of 1787* (New Haven, Conn., 1911), I: 342.

[2]Ibid., I: 305.

[3]John P. Roche, "The Convention as a Case Study in Democratic Politics," *Essays on the Making of the Constitution*, ed. Leonard W. Levy (New York, 1969), 186–97; Edmund S. Morgan, *The Birth of the Republic*, rev. ed. (Chicago, 1977), 139–40; Alfred H. Kelly and Winfred A. Harbison, *The American Constitution: Its Origin and Development*, 3d ed. (New York, 1963), 130; Clinton Rossiter, *1787: The Grand Convention* (New York, 1967), 183–94; Staughton Lynd, *Class Conflict, Slavery and the United States Constitution* (New York, 1967), 153–83, 185–213; Forrest McDonald, *The Formation of the American Republic, 1776–1790* (Baltimore, Md., 1968), 169–70; Peter S. Onuf, *The Origins of the Federal Republic: Jurisdictional Controversies in the United States, 1775–1787* (Philadelphia, 1983), 171–72.

they do not take seriously the primary terms in which participants themselves viewed the conflict: the language of state size.

Because calculations about space, distance, and physical size do not figure largely in our understanding of American politics today, it is easy to overlook their importance in earlier times. Although other divisions in the early republic—the persistence of Court and Country distinctions, the emergence of sectional tensions, and the origins of the two-party system—are all seen as fit subjects for historical analysis, the large- and small-state alliances have been dismissed as transient groupings not worthy of serious attention. Yet such a view fails to comprehend a crucial aspect of political life in the young United States.

For Americans of the time, size was a political issue. Americans conceived of representation in spatial terms and thought spatially about representation questions. A sensitive reading of the Convention debates shows that delegates from states of different sizes had fundamentally different approaches to representation. This fact becomes even more evident when the Philadelphia debate is placed in the context of other debates over representation occurring at both the state and national levels. Emerging before the federal Convention and persisting long after it, the large-state–small-state split was at the heart of the politics of size.

Until the Revolution, Americans took their ideas and institutions of representative government for granted. Although the colonists had borrowed British institutions, adapted them to suit their particular circumstances, and changed them over time, they rarely scrutinized the assumptions behind their notions of representation. Only after attaining independence did they begin to reexamine and reevaluate those assumptions.

After 1776, Americans altered the theory, structure, and function of representative institutions in their states and later in the nation. They changed their laws specifying who could vote as well as who could be elected; separated the functions of the legislative, executive, and judicial branches; demanded greater accountability from their representatives by insisting on frequent elections and rotation in office; equalized representation by changing the basis of apportionment; and devised a theory that explained how representative governments could function in an immense country. Furthermore, they had to construct representative institutions that could accommodate a diverse, geographically mobile population.

Representation lay at the center of the republican experiment. "Representation, the source of American and English liberty, was a thing not understood in its full extent till very lately," said Edmund Randolph in

1788.[4] Innovations in representation distinguished the American government from all others. "The difference most relied on between the American and other republics," observed James Madison in *Federalist* No. 63, "consists in the principle of representation, which is the pivot on which the former move, and which is supposed to have been unknown to the latter."[5] Its importance could not be overestimated. "Virtuous and intelligent representation," concluded a writer in the *New-York Packet* in 1788, "is the mainspring of happiness, and the only proper path of American glory."[6]

Historians, too, have acknowledged the centrality of representation in the early republic. Most studies of this subject fall into two broad categories, which can be called the institutional and the ideological schools. The institutional approach, exemplified in works by J. R. Pole, Elisha P. Douglass, Willi Paul Adams, and Fletcher M. Green, concentrates on the concrete changes in American representative government and on the particular political situations that generated those changes.[7] The ideological school, exemplified in studies by Caroline Robbins, Bernard Bailyn, and Gordon S. Wood, emphasizes the intellectual heritage that shaped American ideas of representation, particularly with reference to the "Real Whig," or Commonwealth, tradition of opposition writings from Great Britain.[8] As valuable as these two approaches are, neither attempts to explore the broader, extrapolitical conditions, created by size itself, that shaped both the theory and the practice of representation in the young United States.[9]

The present book borrows from both the institutional and ideological

---

[4]Jonathan Elliot, ed., *The Debates in the Several State Conventions on the Adoption of the Federal Constitution* . . . (Washington, D.C., 1937), III: 199.

[5]Alexander Hamilton, John Jay, and James Madison, *The Federalist*, ed. Jacob E. Cooke (Middletown, Conn., 1961; orig. publ. 1788), 427.

[6]"Extract from a Letter from One of the Members of the Convention of This State at Poughkeepsie," *New-York Packet*, July 11, 1788.

[7]J.R. Pole, *Political Representation in England and the Origins of the American Republic* (New York, 1966); Elisha P. Douglass, *Rebels and Democrats: The Struggle for Equal Political Rights and Majority Rule during the American Revolution* (Chicago, 1955); Willi Paul Adams, *The First American Constitutions: Republican Ideology and the Making of the State Constitutions of the Revolutionary Era* (Chapel Hill, N.C., 1980); Fletcher M. Green, *Constitutional Development in the South Atlantic States, 1776–1860* (Chapel Hill, N.C., 1930).

[8]Caroline Robbins, *The Eighteenth-Century Commonwealthmen: Studies in the Transmission, Development, and Circumstances of English Liberal Thought from the Restoration of Charles II until the war with the Thirteen Colonies* (Cambridge, Mass., 1967); Bernard Bailyn, *The Ideological Origins of the American Revolution* (Cambridge, Mass., 1967); Gordon S. Wood, *The Creation of the American Republic, 1776–1787* (New York, 1969).

[9]An excellent book that does attempt this kind of analysis, though not specifically with regard to representation, is Onuf's *Origins of the Federal Republic*. In his study of jurisdictional controversies in the United States between 1775 and 1787, Onuf shows how con-

schools but also attempts to do something more: to reconstruct the assumptions that influenced American representative government and to demonstrate how space itself shaped the development of government during its crucial formative period. This book does not pretend to be a chronological or comprehensive history of representation in the United States or an exhaustive account of the way Americans dealt with the problem of size. Rather, it juxtaposes more familiar representation controversies, such as apportionment in the state legislatures, the conflict between large and small states at the federal Convention, and the exchange between Federalists and Antifederalists over an extended republic, with lesser-known debates, such as the discussions about state capital removal, the decision on whether to elect congressmen and presidential electors by districts or at large, and the decennial debates over reapportionment in Congress. Taken together, these controversies reveal an underlying pattern. If, as I believe, Americans started out thinking about representation primarily in spatial terms, their experience during these decades convinced them to modify, and eventually abandon, this view. They began to think about representation in demographic terms—in terms of population rather than territory. This conception endures to the present day.

Although this book is both a political history and a social history of ideas, it finds its inspiration in the study of human geography, a field that explores the connection between the physical environment and political beliefs. Space, according to geographers, is much more than a passive backdrop to human behavior; it actively shapes economic choices, social relationships, and political sympathies. Mental maps— people's perceptions of their physical environment—continually affect the way people see and structure their world.[10] In the early republic, Americans were aware of and articulate about the influence of space on representation issues.

cepts such as "statehood" and "union" affected the political interactions between and among states until the writing of the U.S. Constitution. An interesting study of the influence of space on politics at the microcosmic level is James Sterling Young's *The Washington Community, 1800–1828* (New York, 1966).

[10]The literature of this field is enormous and seldom consulted by historians. It is, however, more useful for its suggestiveness than for any direct application of methodologies. See, for example, David R. Reynolds and Michael L. McNulty, "On the Analysis of Political Boundaries as Barriers: A Perceptual Approach," *Politics and Geographic Relationships: Toward a New Focus*, ed. W. A. Jackson and Marwyn Samuels (Englewood Cliffs, N.J., 1971), esp. 211–13; Jean Gottman, *The Significance of Territory* (Charlottesville, Va., 1973); Paul Ward English, "Landscape, Ecosystem and Environmental Perception: Concepts in Cultural Geography," *Journal of Geography*, 67 (1968), 198–205; Peter R. Gould, "On Mental Maps," in *Michigan Inter-University Community of Mathematical Geographers*, Discussion Paper No. 9, ed. John D. Nystuen (Ann Arbor, Mich., 1966), 1–53;

During and immediately after the Revolution, citizens faced the challenge of extending republican government to the vast territory they had inherited from Great Britain. In fact, most of the individual states—as well as the nation as a whole—were larger than the optimum size recommended for republics by Montesquieu and other political thinkers. Yet, as Americans structured their representative institutions, a distinction emerged between states of different sizes. States that regarded themselves as small faced a different set of demographic problems, issues, and possibilities than states that were considered large.

Legislators in states having a limited area confronted a rather static population. Residents had no large tracts of land into which to move; settlement tended to be compact; the population was fairly homogeneous. As a result, legislators in these states tinkered with, rather than radically reformed, their representative institutions. Approaching representation questions in much the same way they always had, they placed their new capitals at spots determined by geographic, rather than demographic, considerations. They continued to base apportionment in their legislatures on geographic units, such as counties, towns, and parishes. They advocated the equal representation of states—as territorial units—at the federal Convention. And once the new federal government was established, they elected their congressmen and presidential electors by general ticket, which, in effect, meant that the whole state rather than a particular, numerically defined district was represented. Their approach to representation issues, which included but was not limited to territorial apportionment, can be called spatial representation.

Legislators in large states, however, faced a new and different set of circumstances. Citizens in these states realized that their representative institutions needed to accommodate a growing population that was expanding throughout large areas. In this context, the old spatial approach to representation seemed outmoded. Mobility made legislators question whether the geographic community was an adequate basis of representation. The very diversity of interests and transience of relations among new settlers seemed to belie the notion that legislators represented stable, monolithic communities. As a result, legislators in the larger states began to experiment with an approach to representation based on

Edward W. Soja, *The Political Organization of Space,* Association of American Geographers Resource Paper No. 8 (Evanston, Ill., 1971); Raimondo Strassoldo, "Centre-Periphery and System-Boundary: Culturological Perspectives," in *Centre and Periphery: Spatial Variation in Politics,* ed. Jean Gottman (Beverly Hills, Calif., 1980), 27–61; Anne Buttimer, "Social Space in Interdisciplinary Perspective," *Geographical Review,* 59 (1969), 417–26; Edward T. Hall, "The Language of Space," *Landscape,* 10 (1960), 41–45; Hugh C. Prince, "Real, Imagined and Abstract Worlds of the Past," in *Progress in Geography,* ed. Christopher Board et al. (London, 1971), 1–86.

a more fluid, dynamic variable: population. They revamped their representative institutions in more fundamental ways than the small states had, placing their new capitals in the states' demographic centers, adopting numerical apportionment in the lower houses of their legislatures, supporting proportional representation for the national legislature at the federal Convention, and electing their congressmen and presidential electors from districts whose boundaries were drawn according to population. The large states' approach to representation, which included but was not limited to numerical apportionment, can be called demographic representation.

The distinction between large and small states erupted into a full-blown conflict whenever national representation questions came to the fore. The controversy first emerged at the federal Constitutional Convention and was ostensibly resolved by the Great Compromise. Yet the division persisted beyond Philadelphia; it followed representatives into the early sessions of Congress. The procedure for selecting presidential electors, the method of electing congressmen, and the decennial reapportionment of the lower house all mobilized alliances based on state size. Resurfacing periodically until the middle of the nineteenth century, the split between the large and small states had a significant impact on congressional as well as sectional politics.

At the same time Americans were making these institutional decisions, supporters and opponents of the Constitution held a wide-ranging discussion on the theoretical possibility of expanding representative government over a large territory. With a willingness to jettison old arrangements not unrelated to the practice of the large states, Federalists rejected traditional assumptions about representation, which had limited the size of a republic. As long as the representation was sound, they said, as long as the kind and quality of the representatives were high, a republic could exist within a region of any size. Because the Federalists had prevailed in the debate over the Constitution, their concept of representation came to exert an enduring influence on the subsequent resolution of all representation questions.

Throughout the antebellum era, Americans made a fundamental assumption about the relationship between state size and population. State size, they believed, provided an index to a state's future population growth. The more territory a state possessed, the larger its population could grow; the smaller the area, the more limited its growth prospects. Later developments in agriculture, technology, and architecture would invalidate this assumption, making it possible to have dense concentrations of people in small areas. But for early Americans, who could not anticipate these innovations, the connection between size and population seemed unquestionable.

Yet state size was not a static concept. Throughout this period, states gained and lost population and new states joined the union. As a result, some formerly large states became small, relative to the others, and some small states became large. Despite such changes, two facts remained constant. First, a core group of states on each side consistently identified themselves as small or large and voted with other similarly sized states on representation issues. Second, and perhaps more important, participants in the representation debates continued to invoke the language of state size, at least until 1850. They presumably believed that this language reflected some deeper reality. Only when Congress legislated the bases of the division out of existence did this language cease.

Through their confrontation with space, Americans ultimately developed a new approach to representation—an approach based on the individual rather than the community, on population rather than territory, and on demography rather than geography. This new perspective did not, like the old, depend on distance, area, or territory for its efficacy. As a result, Americans could face their large nation with confidence rather than anxiety. In the end, the rejection of spatial assumptions about representation paved the way for virtually unlimited territorial expansion.

CHAPTER 1

The Centrality of

State Capitals

After declaring independence, Americans confronted the dilemmas of extensiveness. Philosophers and political theorists had long asserted that every form of government was suited to a territory of a particular size. According to the eighteenth century Italian philosopher Cesare Beccaria, "Political societies, like the human body, have their limits circumscribed, which they cannot exceed without disturbing their oeconomy."[1] Even the smallest of the former colonies, however, covered an area much larger than that recommended for republican government. The optimum size of a republic, though never defined in exact terms, fell within a narrow range, usually described in terms of a city-state. A larger republic, it was feared, would inevitably deteriorate into anarchy or despotism. A republic that is too large, claimed Montesquieu, "is ruined by an internal imperfection"—by corruption from within.[2] As Americans opened up more and more land for settlement, they had to find a way to resolve the apparent contradiction between republican government and a vast territory.

Inspired by revolutionary ideals of equality and natural rights, citizens wrote new state constitutions and reshaped their institutions of representative government. In doing so, they became concerned with equalizing representation in the legislature, making sure that all parts of the

[1]Marquis Cesare Beccaria, *An Essay on Crimes and Punishment*, 4th ed. (London, 1775), in *America's Italian Founding Fathers*, ed. Adolph Caso (Boston, 1975), 96.

[2]Charles-Louis de Secondat, Baron de Montesquieu, *The Spirit of Laws*, ed. David Wallace Carrithers and trans. Thomas Nugent (Berkeley, Calif., 1977; orig. publ. 1748), 183.

8

state had spokesmen for their interests. Although this process proceeded differently in each state, it involved two distinct methods. The better-known procedure consisted of reapportioning the legislature in proportion to population. In fact, however, in the quarter-century after the Revolution, less than half the original thirteen states adopted this method. A more widespread but less recognized approach entailed removing a state's capital to a more central location. Equal access to the assembly, it was thought, would facilitate more equal representation in the legislature.[3]

During the process of removal itself, a new factor—a state's size—began to play a crucial role in the deliberations. Capitals, it appeared, could be relocated to the state's geographic center or its demographic center. As legislators contemplated the choice, they considered factors such as distance to the seat of government, the prospect of subsequent removals, and, most importantly, the size and distribution of the population. Yet legislators in states having a great deal of territory weighted these factors differently from those in states having little territory. A pattern emerged: small states placed their new capitals at the geographic center; large states situated theirs at the demographic center.

Demands for Removal

Although the removal movement flourished for only a brief period, it was remarkably successful. From 1776 to 1812, citizens in all the original thirteen states agitated for removal of their state capitals to more central locations. In nine of them, they succeeded in permanently shifting the capital. In two others, they developed a system of rotating capitals. As

---

[3]To the extent that they have discussed capital removal at all, historians have seen it simply as part of the ongoing struggle between East and West. They have failed to see it as a conflict over representation. See, for example, Frederick Jackson Turner, "The Old West," in Turner, *The Frontier in American History* (New York, 1920), 121; Merrill Jensen, *The New Nation: A History of the United States during the Confederation, 1781–1789* (New York, 1950), 327–29; Jackson Turner Main, *Political Parties before the Constitution* (Chapel Hill, N.C., 1973), 355; Fletcher M. Green, *Constitutional Development in the South Atlantic States, 1776–1860* (Chapel Hill, N.C., 1930), 164–66. For more general discussions of capital cities, see O. H. K. Spate, "Factors in the Development of Capital Cities," *Geographical Review*, 32 (1942), 622–31; James H. Bird, *Centrality and Cities* (London, 1977); David Lowenthal, "The West Indies Chooses a Capital," in *The Structure of Political Geography*, ed. Roger E. Kasperson and Julian V. Minghi (Chicago, 1969), 350–65; Dieter Prokop, "Image and Functions of the City: An Essay on Social Space," in *Urban Core and Inner City*, Proceedings of the International Study Week, Amsterdam (Leiden, The Netherlands, 1967), 22–34; Raimondo Strassoldo, "Centre-Periphery and System-Boundary: Culturological Perspectives," in *Centre and Periphery: Spatial Variation in Politics*, ed. Jean Gottman (Beverly Hills, Calif., 1980), 27–61.

historian David Ramsay commented in 1808, "The seat of Government was originally on or near the seacoast; but in all of them whose territory reached to the western mountains, in proportion as their population increased in that direction, there has been an eagerness to remove the seat of government so as to approximate the geographical centre of their territories."[4] The migration of settlers westward was soon followed by the removal of state capitals.

In both the states and the nation, removal was one way to ease the problems caused by extensive size. James Madison pointed out during the debates over the national capital, "It has been asserted by some, and almost feared by others, that within so great a space, no free Government can exist. . . . It is incumbent on those who [support republican government] to diminish this inconvenience as much as possible. The way to diminish it, is to place the Government in that spot which will be least removed from every part of the empire."[5] Rather than allow market forces or simple expediency to dictate the sites for their capitals, legislators explicitly sought to locate the site that would best serve the citizens' needs.

It had not always been so. Throughout the colonial period, legislatures had met in coastal cities such as Boston, New York, Philadelphia, and Charles Town. In a few colonies, inland inhabitants made some attempt to move their capitals. Maryland's capital, for example, was relocated in 1694 from St. Mary's to Annapolis.[6] Virginians shifted their capital in 1699 from Jamestown to Williamsburg, although a fire at the capitol in 1747 led to further demands for removal. Reviewing the situation, a House committee agreed that Williamsburg was "very remote from the far greatest Part of the Inhabitants of this Colony."[7] Nevertheless, no removal bill was passed and the capital remained where it was for the time being. In 1746 the North Carolina assembly debated the desirability of moving the seat of government from New Bern to Bath.[8] Although the proposal failed, it was the first in a series of attempts to dislodge the capital from its traditional home.

[4]David Ramsay, *History of South-Carolina, from Its First Settlement in 1670 to the Year 1808* (Newberry, S.C., 1858; orig. publ. 1808), II: 241.

[5]*The Debates and Proceedings in the Congress of the United States* (Washington, D.C., 1834), I: 862 (hereafter cited as *Annals of Congress*). Two versions of this series, both containing identical information on the title pages, were printed in 1834. One version has the running head "Gales and Seaton's History of Debates in Congress"; the other has the running head "History of Congress." The type and pagination of the two series differ. In this book, the "History of Congress" version is used.

[6]Derwent Whittlesey, *The Earth and the State* (New York, 1951), 521.

[7]H. R. McIlwaine, *Journals of the House of Burgesses of Virginia, 1742–1747, 1748–1749* (Richmond, Va., 1909), 242, 244, 247, 283–84; Ivor Noel Hume, *Martin's Hundred: The Discovery of a Lost Colonial Virginia Settlement* (New York, 1983), 27.

[8]Hugh Williamson, *The History of North-Carolina* (Philadelphia, 1812), II: 58–59.

The Revolutionary War loosened the seacoast's monopoly on the seats of government. During the war, newly constituted state assemblies, as well as the Continental Congress, became peripatetic, shifting their meeting sites from place to place to avoid capture by the British. Inland towns were much less vulnerable to surprise attack than the coastal areas and thus became the representatives' favored sites. The New York legislature, for example, moved from New York City to Poughkeepsie, Kingston, and Albany.[9] Leaving their traditional seat of government at New Bern, North Carolina delegates met at various times in Hillsborough, Halifax, and the Wake County Courthouse.[10] Even more mobile than most, the New Hampshire assembly shuttled between Portsmouth, Exeter, Concord, Hopkinton, Dover, Amherst, Charlestown, and Hanover.[11] Although most legislators probably regarded the moves as temporary wartime necessities, many soon became aware of the greater convenience and fairness provided by centrally located seats of government.

After the war, large numbers of Americans began settling the lands beyond the Appalachian Mountains, moving farther and farther away from the traditional seats of government. The territory that became Kentucky, for example, had fewer than a thousand settlers before 1780; by the mid-1790s, it boasted nearly a hundred thousand, and became a state in 1792. The Cumberland region, first settled in the late 1770s, claimed around fifty thousand residents within ten years.[12] The first postrevolutionary generation occupied more new territory than all the previous settlers on the American continent. (See maps 1, 2, and 3.)

As the number of inland settlers increased, so did objections to the eastern capitals. Demands for removal reached a crescendo in the 1780s and 1790s. Although Delaware and Virginia had passed permanent removal statutes during the Revolution, the other states had not.[13] Some

[9]Edgar A. Werner, *Civil List and Constitutional History of the Colony and State of New York* (Albany, N.Y., 1884), 313–21.

[10]Alonzo Thomas Dill, *Governor Tyron and His Palace* (Chapel Hill, N.C., 1955), 244–45; Samuel A. Ashe, *David Paton: Architect of the North Carolina State Capitol*, publication of the North Carolina Historical Commission, Bulletin No. 4 (n.p., 1909), 3–4.

[11]George Barstow, *The History of New Hampshire* (Boston, 1853), 341; James O. Lyford, ed., *History of Concord, New Hampshire* (Concord, N.H., 1903), II: 1091.

[12]Herman R. Friis, "A Series of Population Maps of the Colonies and the United States, 1625–1790," *Geographical Review*, 30 (1940), 463–70; Fulmer Mood, "Studies in the History of American Settled Areas and Frontier Lines: Settled Areas and Frontier Lines, 1625–1790," *Agricultural History*, 26 (1952), 32; J. Potter, "The Growth of Population in America, 1700–1860," in *Population in History*, ed. D. V. Glass and D. E. C. Eversley (London, 1965), 640, 662–63; Gilbert Imlay, *A Topographical Description of the Western Territory of North America* (New York, 1793), I: 79–80.

[13]*Laws of the State of Delaware* (New-Castle, Del., 1777), II: 619–20; William Waller Hening, comp., *The Statutes at Large; Being a Collection of Laws of Virginia* (Richmond, Va., 1822), X: 85–89.

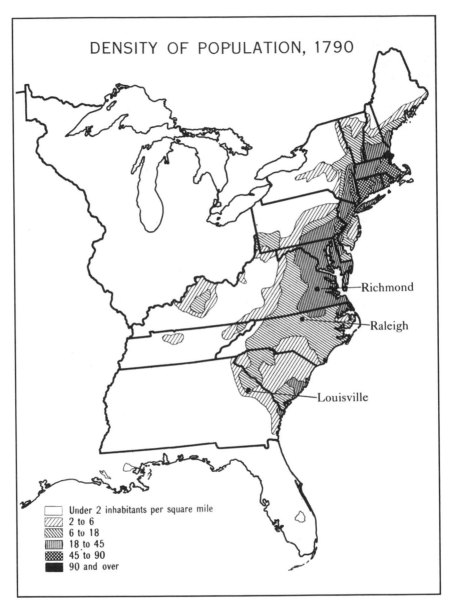

Map 1. Density of population, 1790, and new demographic capitals, 1776–1790

SOURCE: Adapted from Charles O. Paullin, *Atlas of the Historical Geography of the United States*, Publication No. 401 (Baltimore, 1932), plate 76B.

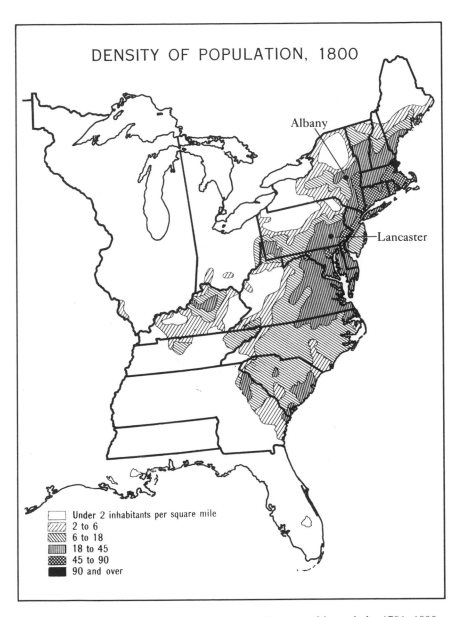

Map 2. Density of population, 1800, and new demographic capitals, 1791–1800

SOURCE: Adapted from Charles O. Paullin, *Atlas of the Historical Geography of the United States*, Publication No. 401 (Baltimore, 1932), plate 76C.

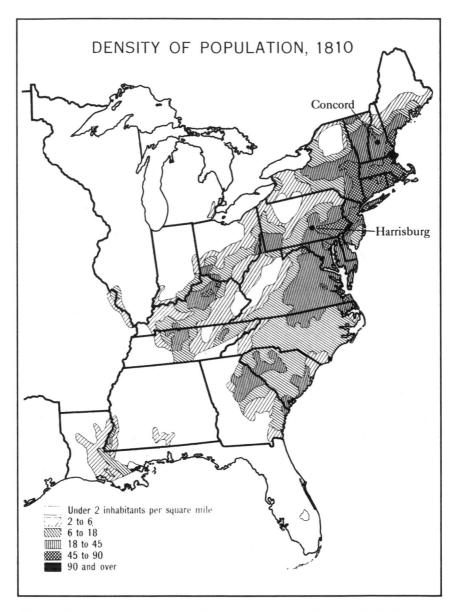

Map 3. Density of population, 1810, and new demographic capitals, 1801–1810

SOURCE: Adapted from Charles O. Paullin, *Atlas of the Historical Geography of the United States*, Publication No. 401 (Baltimore, 1932), plate 76D.

state legislatures had returned to their former homes; others continued to alternate their meeting places. By the 1780s, however, the advantages of an inland capital were apparent. In March 1785, for example, residents of the Little River District in South Carolina sent a petition to their assembly arguing that "the Seat of Government is very inconvenient on account of loss of time and expence . . . to those Inhabitants who are obliged to attend on public or private business." They asked that the capital be relocated "as near the Center of the State as the Legislature may see fit."[14] During Shays's Rebellion in western Massachusetts, insurgents frequently listed "the Sitting of the General Court in Boston" as a grievance.[15] Even those living in states where the capital rotated from place to place wanted the issue settled once and for all. They objected to the "great expense, risque and trouble" involved in constantly moving the legislature as well as official documents from place to place.[16] A permanent capital would add legitimacy as well as stability to the state government, ending the problem of "the Flying State-House."[17]

Between 1776 and 1812, all but two of the states shifted their capitals. (See appendix 1.) After much contention, South Carolina transferred its seat of government in 1786 from Charleston to Columbia.[18] In North Carolina, a convention of the people meeting in 1788 ordered that the capital be moved; it took four more years for the legislature to pass the enabling legislation.[19] Acting more expeditiously, New Jersey abandoned its dual capitals at Burlington and Perth Amboy in 1790 in favor of a single capital at Trenton.[20] New Yorkers, after many years of controversy, agreed in 1797 to move their seat of government from New York

[14]Lark Emerson Adams, ed., *Journals of the House of Representatives, 1785–1786* (Columbia, S.C., 1979), 195.

[15]*Worcester Magazine* (Massachusetts), Fourth Week in August 1786, 247; Third Week in September 1786, 295.

[16]*Farmer's Museum* (Walpole, N.H.), June 13, 1806.

[17]*Osborne's New-Hampshire Spy* (Portsmouth), June 23, 1790.

[18]Adams, *Journals of the South Carolina House*, 573, 596; *Acts, Ordinances and Resolves of the General Assembly of the State of South-Carolina* (Charleston, 1786), 56–58; Francis N. Thorpe, comp., *The Federal and State Constitutions, Colonial Charters, and Other Organic Laws of the States, Territories, and Colonies Now or Heretofore Forming the United States of America* (Washington, D.C., 1909), VI: 3260, 3265; David Duncan Wallace, *South Carolina: A Short History, 1520–1948* (Columbia, S.C., 1961), 342–43.

[19]Walter Clark, ed., *The State Records of North Carolina, 1776–1790* (Goldsboro, N.C., 1903), XXII: 28–29, 33; *State Gazette of North Carolina* (Edenton), September 8, 1788; *Journal of the House of Commons of North Carolina, 1792–1793* (Edenton, 1793), 11, 14, 53, 59; *Journal of the Senate of North Carolina, 1792* (Edenton, 1792), 9, 13, 20, 43, 47, 49; *Laws of North Carolina . . . First Session, 1792* (n.p., 1792), 7–8.

[20]William Paterson, comp., *Laws of the State of New-Jersey* (Newark, 1800), 104; Richard P. McCormick, *Experiment in Independence: New Jersey in the Critical Period, 1781–1789* (New Brunswick, N.J., 1950), 125–26.

City to Albany.[21] In New Hampshire, although the official removal act did not pass until 1816, Concord became the state's de facto capital after 1808.[22]

Some states even moved their capitals more than once. Georgia, for example, shifted its seat of government from Savannah to Louisville in 1786, with an interim capital at Augusta. By 1804, however, the western parts of the state had become so populous that another removal was called for—this time to Milledgeville.[23] Pennsylvanians relocated their seat of government from Philadelphia to Lancaster in 1799 and then from Lancaster to Harrisburg in 1810.[24] Two states continued the practice of rotating their capitals well into the nineteenth century. The Rhode Island assembly traveled from Newport to Providence to East Greenwich to South Kingston and Bristol, and the Connecticut delegation alternated between Hartford and New Haven.[25] Only the legislatures of Massachusetts and Maryland refused to accede to the demands for removal during this period. Yet even they experienced intense agitation concerning the matter.[26]

[21]*Journal of the Assembly of the State of New-York* (Albany, 1797), 89–90, 108; *Laws of the State of New-York, Comprising the Constitution and Acts of Legislature, since the Revolution, from the First to the Twentieth Session, Inclusive* (New York, 1797), III: 391–93; *Diary* (New York), February 14, 1797.

[22]Eliphalet Merrill and Phinehas Merrill, *Gazetteer of the State of New-Hampshire* (Exeter, N.H., 1817), 102; Barstow, *History of New Hampshire*, 341; Lyford, *History of Concord, New Hampshire*, II: 1091; *Laws of New Hampshire* (Concord, 1920), VIII: 525.

[23]Allen D. Chandler, comp., *The Colonial Records of the State of Georgia* (Atlanta, 1911), III: 466–68; Clark Howell, *History of Georgia* (Chicago, 1926), I: 443–44; T. S. Arthur and W. H. Carpenter, *The History of Georgia, from Its Earliest Settlement to the Present Time* (Philadelphia, 1853), 310–11; Augustin Smith Clayton, comp., *A Compilation of the Laws of the State of Georgia, Passed by the Legislature since the Political Year 1800, to the Year 1810, Inclusive* (Augusta, 1812), 100–7, 209–10, 265–66.

[24]*Journal of the First Session of the Ninth House of Representatives of Pennsylvania, 1798–1799* (Philadelphia, 1799), 127, 366–68, 378, 383, 391; *Journal of the Senate of the Commonwealth of Pennsylvania* (Philadelphia, 1798), IX: 232, 256–60; *Bache's Philadelphia Aurora*, April 1, 1799; *Journal of the Twentieth House of Representatives of the Commonwealth of Pennsylvania* (Lancaster, 1809), 351, 443, 445, 453–56, 472, 482–83, 491–92; *Journal of the Senate of the Commonwealth of Pennsylvania* (Lancaster, 1809), XX: 78, 121, 177, 188–89, 559.

[25]Connecticut continued the practice until 1873, when the permanent capital was established at Hartford. Rhode Island persisted until 1900, when Providence was made the single seat of government. Forrest Morgan, *Connecticut as a Colony and As a State, or One of the Original Thirteen* (Hartford, Conn., 1904), 134–35; Edward Field, *State of Rhode Island and Providence Plantation at the End of the Century: A History* (Boston, 1902), I: 390–91.

[26]Although Maryland's capital had been moved from St. Mary's to Annapolis in 1694, an intense—and ultimately unsuccessful—struggle developed in the 1780s over whether it should be moved again, this time to Baltimore. In Massachusetts, participants in Shays's Rebellion listed the capital's location as a specific grievance. See A. C. Hanson [Aristides], *Considerations on the Proposed Removal of the Seat of Government, Addressed to the Citizens of Maryland* (Annapolis, Md., 1786); *Worcester Magazine*, Fourth Week in August 1786, 247; ibid., Third Week in September 1786, 295; *Independent Gazetteer* (Philadelphia), March 9, 1787.

Distance and Representation

During the revolutionary era, when Americans first began to think about the problems of equal representation, they focused primarily on the issue of equal access. The other alternative—reapportionment on the basis of population—was a new, untried system of governance that required fundamental institutional change. If citizens were reluctant to tamper with corporate representation, legislators themselves were even more resistant, because they had a direct stake in the old system. Physically removing the capital, however, seemed to be an easier way for legislators to address the representation question while at the same time logically extending common assumptions about how representative government should work.

Petitions for removal often listed the time, expense, and difficulty of travel to the capital as reasons for shifting the seat of government. Over and over, they stressed that for "the ease & Convenience of the Community at large" the capitals should be moved from their "inconvenient" locations on the states' peripheries.[27] Yet distance from the seat of government caused more than annoyance; it actually determined a section's ability to send representatives to the assembly.

The demands for removal were based not just on a desire to minimize the difficulty of travel to the capital but also on a principled awareness of what those distances implied for representation. If the difficulty of travel had prompted the outrage, then, as one Pennsylvania legislator proposed, "Good roads from one end of the state to the other, will be found a much better means of reducing the inconvenience of the distance to the seat of government."[28] Yet citizens wanted more than good roads. If distance alone had been the problem, residents of smaller states would not have demanded removal, or would have demanded it less frequently than those in larger states, because they had far shorter distances to travel to their seats of government. But as James Madison observed in 1790, "In every instance where the seat of Government has been placed in an uncentral position, we have seen the people struggling to place it where it *ought to be*" (emphasis added).[29] Americans believed that it was a matter of right, not simply of personal comfort, to have a centrally located capital. As Virginia's removal statute noted, "The equal rights of

[27]Adams, *Journals of the South Carolina House*, 26–27. See also ibid., 140, 331; *Laws of Delaware*, II: 619–20; *Farmer's Cabinet* (Amherst, N.H.), June 7, 1806; Hanson, *Considerations on Removal in Maryland*, 4; *Carlisle Gazette* (Carlisle, Pa.), March 28, 1787.

[28]"Extracts from Mr. Brackenridge's Address on Findley's Motion," *Independent Gazetteer*, August 15, 1787.

[29]*Annals of Congress*, I: 861–62.

all the said inhabitants require that such seat of government should be as nearly central to all [as possible]."[30]

When petitioners demanded a more conveniently located capital, they meant more than personal convenience. Their notion of convenience had a public dimension. Certainly large distances caused problems for individuals who had to attend court, pay taxes, or register land claims at the capital. Yet these concerns affected only a small minority.

The most important consequence of large distances affected representation in the legislature. Outlying areas simply could not send their full share of representatives to meetings of the assembly and therefore were not fully represented. A more centrally located capital would help rectify that situation. A Maryland writer calling himself "Aristides" observed that Maryland's constitution ordered "that the place for the meeting of the legislature must be the most convenient to the members." This clause, he argued "means a place the most central, the most convenient for them to repair to, and best suited to them *in their public characters, as members of the legislature*" (emphasis added).[31] For Americans living in the eighteenth century, the word *convenient* meant something close to its Latin root: "coming together, uniting."[32] Large distances in effect prevented the people's representatives from convening together to make laws for society. A more conveniently located capital meant one that would be more accessible to legislators in all parts of the state.

The desire for physical proximity to the seat of government flowed naturally from the distinctively American notion of actual representation. The colonists had explicitly rejected the British notion of virtual representation, which stipulated that elected legislators speak for the community's common good. In contrast, actual representation implied that the legislature should be a microcosm of the larger society—that legislators should reflect the particular needs, wishes, and desires of those who elected them. As the "Essex Result" noted in 1778, "The rights of representation should be so equally and impartially distributed, that the representatives should have the same views, and interests with the people at large. They should think, feel, and act like them, and in fine, should be an exact miniature of their constituents."[33] Representa-

---

[30]Hening, *Statutes at Large*, X: 85–89.

[31]Hanson, *Considerations on Removal in Maryland*, 54.

[32]*The Compact Edition of the Oxford English Dictionary*, s.v. "convenient"; Garry Wills, *Confessions of a Conservative* (New York and Middlesex, England, 1979), 57–58.

[33]"Theophilus Parsons," "Essex Result" (Newburyport, Mass., 1778), in *American Political Writing during the Founding Era, 1760–1805*, ed. Charles S. Hyneman and Donald S. Lutz (Indianapolis, 1983), I: 497. See also Bernard Bailyn, *The Ideological Origins of the American Revolution* (Cambridge, Mass., 1967), 160–75; Gordon S. Wood, *The Creation of the American Republic* (New York, 1969), 173–88, 363–72.

tive government was considered a poor but necessary substitute for the personal participation of all the electors in the law-making process.

The insistence on actual representation had fueled the constitutional crisis surrounding the Stamp Act and had hastened the coming of the Revolution. What historians have failed to emphasize, however, is the spatial dimension implicit in actual representation. Virtual representation had no physical constraints; it could be extended to encompass a society of any size or area. Attacking the American rejection of virtual representation, Englishman Soame Jenyns asked, "Why does not this . . . [parliamentary] representation extend to America as well as over the whole Island of Great Britain? If it can travel three hundred miles, why not three thousand? if it can jump over rivers and mountains, why cannot it sail over the ocean?"[34] In contrast, actual representation could exist only within relatively small areas. The confidence of people in their government rested on people's ability to know and be known by their representatives. "The members of our State legislatures . . . are chosen within small circles," observed an Antifederalist in 1788. "They are sent but a small distance from their respective homes: Their conduct is constantly known to their constituents. They frequently see, and are seen by the men whose servants they are. . . . They return, and mix with their neighbours of the lowest rank, see their poverty, and feel their wants."[35] The compactness of early American settlement reinforced the American tendency toward localism in representation.

The Real Whig tradition also promoted the notion of close contact between representatives and constituents. As inheritors of this ideology, Americans viewed their legislatures with suspicion. Only vigilance, guaranteed through physical proximity, could safeguard liberty. It was essential, asserted Samuel Adams, that the people "acquaint themselves with the Character and Conduct of those who represent them at the distance of four hundred Miles. . . . What do frequent Elections avail, without that Spirit of Jealousy and Strict Inquiry which alone can render such Elections any Security to the People?"[36] If the people did not supervise their representatives closely, their representatives might, as a Pennsylvanian put it, "pass laws . . . touching the life, liberty and property of the citizens before any steps could be taken to evade the evil."[37]

[34]Soame Jenyns, "The Objections to the Taxation of Our American Colonies by the Legislature of Great Britain, Briefly Consider'd" (London, 1765), in *Sources and Documents Illustrating the American Revolution, 1764–1788, and the Formation of the Federal Constitution,* ed. Samuel Eliot Morison, 2d ed. (New York and London, 1979), 20.

[35]"Cornelius," in *The Complete Anti-Federalist,* ed. Herbert J. Storing with the editorial assistance of Murray Dry (Chicago, 1981), IV: 141.

[36]Samuel Adams to John Adams, December 8, 1777, in *The Writings of Samuel Adams,* ed. Harry Alonzo Cushing (New York, 1907), III: 416.

[37]*Independent Gazetteer,* March 9, 1787.

Like the use of binding instructions, extralegal conventions, mobbing, and electioneering, the movement to relocate the seats of government can be seen as a part of what historian Gordon Wood calls the postrevolutionary "breakdown of confidence between the people-at-large and their representative governments."[38] If the capital were more centrally located, all the people in the state would have a better opportunity to make their wishes known to the legislature and to see that those wishes were carried out.

Distance inevitably influenced the kind, quality, and quantity of representation that people in different parts of the state received. The farther a resident lived from the capital, the more limited was the person's information about government, especially in legislative matters. Inhabitants of outlying regions depended largely on word-of-mouth to keep them informed about the government. Whereas citizens living in or near urban centers could rely on newspapers for political information, back-country inhabitants often received no newspapers at all or received them only after delays of two weeks to two months. "*Knowledge* & the proper *Circulation* thereof, I take to be the very Essence of Republican Government," wrote a Pennsylvanian to Benjamin Rush in 1784. "How is it, then, that the Proceedings of Assembly are rarely, if ever, communicated in the *back* Parts of the State, 'till the Session is over?"[39] Even then, newspapers at the time tended to concentrate on national and foreign news at the expense of state and local information.[40]

Large distances also limited the ability of representatives to understand their constituents. State representatives might become as insensitive to the people as the English government had become to the colonists before the Revolution. A resident of the New Hampshire Grants region, for example, noted in 1777 that were his territory to be governed by New York State, "the State would be so large, that gentlemen from the extreme parts would not personally know but very little better the situation of the other extreme parts than a gentleman would from London."[41] In 1780, inhabitants of Bedford County, Virginia, expressed a common suspicion, remarking, "From our remote situation, we are always liable to be imposed on by our assessors."[42] Lurking

[38]Wood, *Creation of the American Republic*, 368.

[39]Quoted in Robert L. Brunhouse, *The Counter-Revolution in Pennsylvania, 1776–1790* (Harrisburg, Pa., 1942), 4.

[40]J. R. Pole, *Political Representation in England and the Origins of the American Republic* (New York, 1966), 285–86; *Independent Gazetteer*, March 8, 1787; Griffith J. McRee, ed., *Life and Correspondence of James Iredell* (New York, 1858), II: 150.

[41]Ira Allen, *Some Miscellaneous Remarks and Short Arguments on a Small Pamphlet . . .* (Hartford, Conn., 1777), 25.

[42]Bedford County Petition, May 23, 1780, in Virginia State Library, Richmond, Va.

behind the calls for removal lay a fear that large distances would breed corruption.

Most importantly, distance discouraged attendance at meetings of the legislature. In large states, such as New York and Pennsylvania, the most distant legislators had to journey hundreds of miles to reach the capital. Even in a small state, such as Delaware, they would have to go fifty-five miles, or the equivalent of a day's travel.[43] Travel in the late eighteenth century was difficult, time-consuming, and expensive. A light stagecoach, for example, could make the trip between New York and Philadelphia in two days, between New York and Boston in three days, and between New York and Baltimore in four to six days.[44] "There are some of the western members [of the legislature]," noted a North Carolinian in 1789, "who live near five hundred miles from the seat of government. When you consider the incidents that attend travelling across mountains in winter, and in bad roads, you must allow those members three or four weeks to come to the seat of government, or to return home."[45] To compound these difficulties, many states did not pay their legislators a salary; others did not even pay their expenses, preferring to let each constituency support its own representatives.[46] Because the cost of supporting a legislator from a remote area might be substantial, many places chose to forgo representation altogether.

Eighteenth century Americans routinely assumed that outlying regions would be less well represented than those nearer the capital. Citizens of Springfield, Massachusetts, commented in 1780, "It is probable, by Reason of their different situations, that many of the more distant Towns will generally omit the full Exercise of their Rights, and that those at or near the Center of Government will exercise them in their full Extent."[47] Distance made illusory the possibility of equal

---

[43]*Journal of the House of Representatives of the State of Delaware* (Newcastle, 1797), 56; William A. Schaper, "Sectionalism and Representation in South Carolina," *Annual Report of the American Historical Association for the Year 1900* (Washington, D.C., 1901), I: 251; Allen, *Some Miscellaneous Remarks*, 8; *Daily Advertiser* (New York), March 13, 1787; *Carlisle Gazette*, May 2, 1787.

[44]Henry Adams, *The United States in 1800* (Ithaca, 1974; orig. publ. 1889), 8–10; Charles O. Paullin, *Atlas of the Historical Geography of the United States*, Publication No. 401 (Baltimore, Md., 1932), plate 138a; Ralph H. Brown, *Mirror for Americans: Likeness of the Eastern Seaboard—1810* (New York, 1943), 43–54.

[45]"Extract of a Letter from Edenton, North Carolina, January 28, 1789," *Providence Gazette, or Country Journal* (Rhode Island), March 21, 1789.

[46]Allan Nevins, *The American States during and after the Revolution, 1775–1789* (New York, 1969), 182; Pole, *Political Representation*, 285–86; Massachusetts Constitution of 1780, *The Popular Sources of Political Authority: Documents on the Massachusetts Constitution of 1780*, ed. Oscar Handlin and Mary Handlin (Cambridge, Mass., 1966), 454.

[47]Statement from Hampshire County, May 29, 1780, in Handlin and Handlin, *Popular Sources*, 607.

representation. Residents of Lenox objected to the Massachusetts constitution of 1778 because, as they put it, "[Article 6] has a tendency to induce the Remote parts of the State . . . to neglect keeping a Representative at the General Court. In a word it is making Representation unequal."[48]

Inequities in the system were commonplace. In 1788, for example, North Carolina's far-eastern counties were less likely than any other region to send their full share of representatives to the legislative session, meeting at Fayetteville in the south-central portion of the state.[49] Inhabitants of Portsmouth, New Hampshire, observed in 1790, "We neglect to improve the privilege to which by our constitution we are entitled, that of sending Representatives to the General Court. In the county of Rockingham, more than one half of the towns are unrepresented, whilst the representation from the upper counties [where the legislature meets] is very full."[50] This pattern continued over time. The county most distant from the assembly's meeting place in 1807 sent the lowest percentage of representatives. Whereas nearby New Hampshire counties sent more than 90 percent of their legislators, Stafford county residents sent only 79 percent of theirs.[51] When distant regions failed to send their assigned number of representatives, an already serious representation problem was made all the worse.

The demands for removal represented a logical expression of spatial assumptions about representation. At a time when reapportionment still seemed like a novelty, removal appeared to be the safer, more traditional alternative. In a political milieu where physical proximity contributed so concretely to the kind, quality, and quantity of representation, relocating the seat of government seemed to be a reasonable method of equalizing representation. With the capital at the state's center, no one section would be able to exert greater pressure or send a larger proportion of representatives than any other. As James Madison noted during

---

[48]Statement from Lenox, May 20, 1778, in Handlin and Handlin, *Popular Sources*, 254.

[49]Counties such as Carteret, Dobbs, Duplin, Hawkins, Moore, Pasquotank, Tyrrel, and Wayne and the town of New Bern failed to send their full share of representatives. Conclusions are based on a comparison of the counties of the representatives present at a vote on removal taken on November 20, 1788, with the list of counties entitled to representation. Clark, *State Records of North Carolina*, XXIII: 1–5, 73–74.

[50]*Osborne's New-Hampshire Spy* (Portsmouth), June 23, 1790.

[51]The legislature was meeting at Hopkinton, in Hillsborough County. Conclusions are based on a comparison of the elected representatives with those in attendance on June 19, 1807, at a vote on removal. The attendance rates were Hillsborough, 91 percent; Rockingham, 90.5 percent; Cheshire, 91 percent; Grafton, 93 percent; and Stafford, 79 percent. The list of representatives can be found in *Concord Gazette* (New Hampshire), June 16, 1807. The vote is in *A Journal of the Proceedings of the House of Representatives of the State of New Hampshire* (Portsmouth, 1807), 95.

the debate over the location of the national capital: "If you place the
Government in an uncentral situation, the attendance of the members,
and of all others who are to transact the public business cannot be
equally convenient. . . . You violate the principle of equality, where it
ought most carefully to be ascertained, and wound the feelings of the
component parts of the community."[52] Removal, it was thought, would
break the East's traditional dominance in the state assemblies. It would
help maintain the necessary degree of intimacy between representatives
and constituents by keeping contacts between the two frequent, mean-
ingful, and financially feasible. For many eighteenth century Americans, equal representation in the legislature meant equal access to the
seat of government.

In Defense of "Metropolitan Honors"

Yet not everyone favored removal. The removal debates were marked
by bitterness and division among the people and their legislators. For
one thing, removal played on the traditional tension between urban and
rural areas. Residents of the interior argued that, among other things,
the country was a much healthier place than the city to hold meetings of
the legislature. In contrast to the dirt, noise, overcrowding, and un-
healthiness of the city, rural capitals offered "salubrious air" and a
"healthy situation."[53] A yellow fever epidemic in Philadelphia, for example, was cited as a good reason to move the legislature to another
location.[54] A North Carolinian put his feelings on the subject into verse:

> A landscape fair thr'out this verdant *Seat*,
> Will furnish here a calm and cool retreat;
> From noxious climes, and summer's sickliest rage,
> For fading youth, and old decrepid age.[55]

Some charged that cities bred legislative corruption by permitting representatives to conduct private business and by allowing them to indulge
themselves in urban pleasures. "As much legislative business may be
transacted in the country in three weeks," claimed a writer from upstate
New York, "as may be done in the city in four, or nearly in that propor-

---

[52]*Annals of Congress*, I: 862.

[53]Quoted in McCormick, *Experiment in Independence*, 126. See also John Clark to Governor Milledge, September 27, 1804, in *Correspondence of John Milledge, Governor of Georgia,
1802–1806*, ed. Harriet Milledge Salley (Columbia, S.C., 1949), 122.

[54]*Pennsylvania House Journal, 1798–1799*, 127.

[55]*North-Carolina Journal* (Halifax), January 9, 1793.

tion."[56] Mobs posed an ever-present threat in large cities. "It is well known," said a Maryland commentator, "that in large and free capitals, the open deliberations of the legislature are liable to interruption from the populace. . . . The state governments of New-York, South-Carolina and Pennsylvania, have all been removed from the great trading cities to places in the interior of the country, principally on account of greater personal safety and freedom of debate."[57] Rural capitals, it was thought, would help alleviate such pressure as well as ensure a more conducive environment for the business at hand.

Not surprisingly, inhabitants of the current capitals dreaded the possibility of removal. After 1780, the specter of Williamsburg haunted the states. Once the Virginia government had left for Richmond, the former capital fell into a precipitous decline. People fled, businesses closed, real estate values plummeted, and "merchants, advocates, and other considerable residents took their departure as well, and the town . . . lost half its population."[58] According to St. George Tucker of Virginia, any city in Williamsburg's situation might well share the same end. "Rome, the mighty mistress of the world, fell as soon as her metropolitan honors were snatched from her, and transferred to Constantinople," he said. "And could Williamsburg expect a better fate when the feeble prop of her existence was removed to Richmond?"[59] Inhabitants of other capital cities also believed that the government provided the "feeble prop" underlying their own existence and prosperity.

Yet, whereas supporters of removal in all the states adhered to certain common principles, opponents of removal offered a wide variety of arguments, even within a single state. In Pennsylvania in 1787, for example, Representative William Findley proposed a motion calling for the removal of the capital from Philadelphia to Lancaster.[60] This action unleashed a torrent of abuse on both him and his proposal. Some accused Findley of seeking private gain through the bill. According to one critic, the people would have to bear additional taxes simply "in order that the member from Westmoreland may not have quite so many miles to ride!"[61] Another author argued that Findley and his supporters "own

---

[56]*Otsego Herald; or, Western Advertiser* (Cooperstown, N.Y.), January 5, 1797.

[57]"A Friend of the People," *Candid Appeal to the Freemen of Maryland on the Projected Removal of Their Seat of Government* (n.p., 1817), 8.

[58]Johann D. Schoepf, in *We Were There: Descriptions of Williamsburg, 1699–1859*, ed. Jane Carson (Charlottesville, Va., 1965), 73.

[59]St. George Tucker, "A letter to the Rev. Jedidiah Morse . . ." (1795), *William & Mary Quarterly*, 1st. ser., 2 (1894), 187–88.

[60]*Independent Gazetteer*, March 8, 1787; March 9, 1787.

[61]*Carlisle Gazette*, March 28, 1787.

all the property in the town and neighborhood of Harrisburg—the offices and influence of government of course would fall into their hands."[62] Still others insisted that Findley had deliberately waited until the session's end, after many members had left, to raise the matter. Rather than being presented to the whole assembly, the subject had been "*stolen* through" without proper consideration or debate.[63]

Other attacks focused on the larger public issues at stake. Moving the capital, some feared, would send the city into a precipitous decline. "Whatever tends to render Philadelphia flourishing and active," said an author calling himself "Civis," "sheds a beneficial influence on the state at large. To withdraw the offices of government from the City may depress its trade and depopulate its streets."[64] A member of the assembly, Henry Hugh Brackenridge, doubted that a removal undertaken at that time would be permanent. Another shift would likely be necessary, causing the taxpayers extra expense and inconvenience.[65] In addition, Brackenridge opposed the particular site that had been offered, saying, "Philadelphia is eccentral, but Harrisburgh is not central."[66] Still others believed that by moving the legislature out of Philadelphia, the people would have less, not more, control over their legislators. One member of the state assembly commented, "While the Assembly sits in this city, every individual in the state is informed of its proceedings, by the circulation of the newspapers which are published here, and in case of any attempt to abridge their privileges, have it in their power to shew their disapprobation, sooner than could be done if it was removed into the country."[67] Despite their vehemence, opponents of removal, like opponents of the U.S. Constitution, had no single rationale to unite them. The absence of a unified opposition no doubt contributed to the widespread success of the removal movement from 1776 to 1812.

Even those who supported removal sometimes disagreed about the precise location for the new capital. Eighteenth century Americans attributed enormous prestige and power to their seats of government. It was believed that the mere honor of hosting the capital would bring a place tremendous gains in population, trade, business, and revenue. "It is presumed," said a Pennsylvania writer, "that wherever the seat of government may be established, if it is a place admitting of commerce, that men of capital will naturally be drawn there to settle."[68] A member

[62]*Independent Gazetteer*, March 8, 1787.
[63]Ibid., March 9, 1787.
[64]*Carlisle Gazette*, March 28, 1787; *Independent Gazetteer*, March 8, 1787.
[65]*Independent Gazetteer*, August 15, 1787.
[66]Ibid.
[67]Ibid., March 8, 1787.
[68]*Poulson's American Daily Advertiser* (Philadelphia), February 2, 1810.

of the South Carolina legislature suggested that the location of the new state capital was immaterial to its growth because "its natural advantages would particularly result from the great resort of strangers and others, who had business to transact with the state officers, or the legislature."[69] "A True Federalist," writing in the *American Museum*, confirmed the assumption: "It is well known that vast importance and advantages with respect to population and riches, are always derived to [the seat of government] and its surrounding districts, where the public revenues are collected into a point, and which is the centre of great monied operations."[70] Summing up a widespread attitude toward capital cities, a North Carolinian commented, "Should the Assembly return hither, our importance is sealed."[71] Because of the high stakes involved, representatives from various towns vied to have the new seat of government located in their districts.

The Ambiguity of Centrality

What all supporters of removal agreed on was that the new seat of government should be centrally located. Centrality, they thought, was the principle of equality expressed in geographic terms. Americans envisioned the republic as a circle and the legislature's meeting place as the center of it. "A nation is not . . . to be represented by the human body," wrote Thomas Paine in *The Rights of Man*, "but it is like the body contained within a circle, having a common centre, in which every radius meets; and that centre is formed by representation."[72] Although the people in a republic might disperse over a large territory, their representatives returned to the center to pass legislation. The natural limit of a republic, said Madison in *Federalist* No. 14, "is that distance from the center which will barely allow the representatives of the people to meet as often as may be necessary for the administration of public affairs."[73] Extending the circle metaphor, Thomas Jefferson saw the center as the source of strength and life for the republic. In his jottings in the margins of Virginia's removal bill, Jefferson noted, "Central

[69]*Charleston Morning Post, and Daily Advertiser* (South Carolina), March 15, 1786.
[70]"A True Federalist," "Considerations on the Future Place of Residence of Congress," *American Museum*, 5 (1789), 182.
[71]McRee, *Life and Correspondence of James Iredell*, II: 126.
[72]Thomas Paine, *The Rights of Man* (New York and Harmondsworth, England, 1979; orig. publ. 1791–1792), 203.
[73]Alexander Hamilton, John Jay, and James Madison, *The Federalist*, ed. Jacob E. Cooke (Middletown, Conn., 1961; orig. publ. 1788), 85.

. . . Heart—Sun—Ch[ur]ch—C[our]thouse.">[74] Just as the heart sustained an individual's life, so the capital was the source of life in a republic. Similarly, just as Virginia's churches and county courthouses represented the focus of local public life, so the seat of government acted as the locus of public activities within the state.

Americans had ample precedent for their emphasis on centrality. Political philosophers with whom they were familiar had long advocated the notion of a centrally situated capital city. Aristotle's *Politics*, for example, described the ideal seat of government as a "common centre, linked to the sea as well as land, and equally linked to the whole of the territory."[75] Frenchman Alexandre Le Maître's 1682 tract, *La Metropolitée*, promoted the notion of a capital fixed in the center of a territory within a highly productive, easily defensible region.[76] Central location was a valued attribute of capital cities.

Legislators soon found, however, that the actual task of locating the center was more complicated than they had at first believed. The concept of centrality was ambiguous. The center could refer to the center of population, wealth, or territory. One congressman despaired: "The principles offered are vague, and lead to no certain conclusion. What is the centre of wealth, population, and territory? Is there a common centre? Territory has one centre, population another, and wealth a third. . . . This was not a practicable mode of settling the place [of government]."[77] As state representatives began to select the precise locations of their new capitals, they too realized that they had to define *centrality*.

As the debates over capitals proceeded, the implications of the different forms of centrality became apparent. Most legislators quickly rejected the notion of a capital in the center of wealth. Such a point would be difficult, if not impossible, to ascertain, and would not redress inequities in representation.[78] The choice was basically between the centers of population and of territory, with each offering distinct benefits and drawbacks.

State size, in terms of area, influenced the location of capitals. Legislators in states with a small amount of territory faced a different set of

[74]"Notes concerning the Bill for the Removal of the Seat of Government of Virginia, 11 November 1776," in *The Papers of Thomas Jefferson*, ed. Julian P. Boyd (Princeton, N.J., 1951–), I: 602.

[75]Aristotle, *The Politics of Aristotle*, trans. Ernest Barker (London, 1974), 307.

[76]Alexandre Le Maître, *La Metropolitée, ou De l'etablissement des villes capitales, de leur utilité passive & active, de L'union de leurs parties & de leur anatomie, de leur commerce, &c.* (Amsterdam, The Netherlands, 1682), 46.

[77]*Annals of Congress*, I: 841.

[78]Ibid.

issues than did legislators in large-territory states. The small states had
populations that were fairly evenly dispersed and boundaries that usually were well-defined and uncontested. Therefore, the legislators
viewed their states as discrete territorial units and selected capital sites
on the basis of geographic factors. New Jersey and Delaware, for example, fixed their seats of government within twenty-five miles of their
states' respective geographic centers. Maryland, another small state, had
already moved its capital to Annapolis, a site very near the state's territorial center.[79] Two other small states, Rhode Island and Connecticut,
continued the practice of alternating the legislature's meeting place from
town to town. (See map 4.)

One advantage of the geographic over the demographic center was the
ease with which it could be determined. By consulting maps, geographies, and reports from surveying expeditions, representatives could
ascertain a state's territorial center with great precision. The members of
a legislative committee in South Carolina reported, for example, that
they had "examined and Compared all the different Maps of the State
which they could possess themselves of, and are of the Opinion that the
Center of the State is included in a Circle whose Circumference strikes
through the High Hills of Santee."[80] Given the paucity of detailed
census data in the early republic, the convenience in determining the
geographic center offered a substantial benefit over the harder to locate
demographic center.

A seat of government placed in the geographic center also offered the
advantage of permanence. Provided boundaries remained the same, the
geographic center would remain stationary. But as the population grew
and settlers moved into new territory, the population center would shift.
"The centre of population is variable," said a U.S. congressman, "and a
decision on that principle now might establish the seat of Government at
a very inconvenient place to the next generation."[81] Population was
growing so rapidly, a Pennsylvanian warned, that "to fix the seat [of
government] at present, regarding only the peopled country, is making a
garment for a youth fitted to his size, which he must outgrow in a short
period. It is fixing the center of gravity of a machine while some of the
parts of which it is to be composed are wanting."[82] Although such

[79]*Geographic centrality* has been defined according to a strict criterion. Only capitals
located within a twenty-five mile radius of the state's exact geographic center have been
considered geographically central. For precise geographic centers, see Edward M. Douglas, *Boundaries, Areas, Geographic Centers and Altitudes of the United States and the Several
States*, Bulletin No. 817, 2d ed. (Washington, D.C., 1932), 254.
[80]Adams, *Journals of the South Carolina House*, 533.
[81]*Annals of Congress*, I: 841.
[82]*Independent Gazetteer*, August 15, 1787.

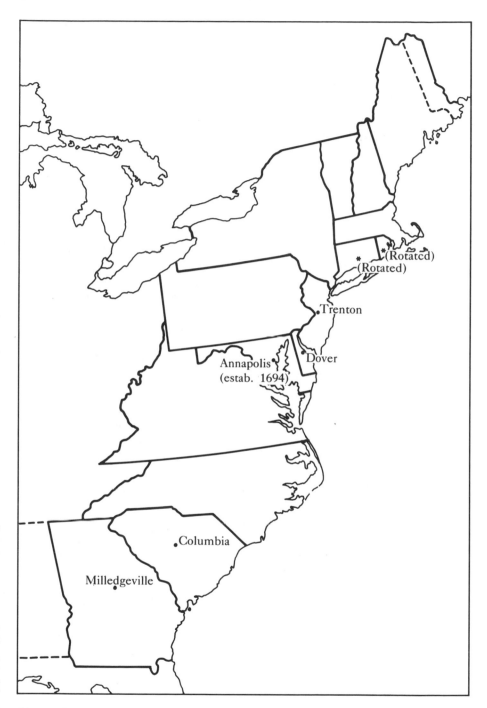

Map 4. Geographic capitals, 1776–1812

population shifts might pose problems in states having large unsettled regions, it did not present a significant difficulty for smaller states that were already settled throughout the extent of their territory.

The rotating capital, although not a fixed point, also reflected a consideration of geographic factors. Having examined the entire territory within their state's boundaries, legislators in Rhode Island and Connecticut selected various sites throughout the states that were convenient to all citizens. Their capitals actually moved from place to place to give representatives and constituents from different parts of the state access to the seat of government.

In contrast, delegates in the larger states tended to place their capitals at the states' demographic centers. They realized that a capital located at the geographic center would not redress the citizens' grievances. Population in these states was widely scattered. Not all regions had yet been settled. Boundaries were often unknown or in dispute. As the legislators made their decisions, they realized that the main advantage of the territorial center, its permanence, also represented its biggest handicap. Although geographic centers were fixed, they did not respond to the needs of people currently inhabiting the state. The centers would often be located, as one congressman put it, in the midst of an "uninhabited Wilderness."[83] But what demographic centers lacked in permanence, they gained in accessibility to all current residents. A delegate to the South Carolina assembly commented in 1786 that he "did not want the central place to be the centre of pine trees; he rather wished they might employ their wisdom in finding out the centre of inhabitants."[84]

Finding the demographic center was difficult but by no means impossible. Although Americans of the early national period did not have modern population distribution maps, they could and did consult tax rolls, voting records, and their own "knowledge of the country,"[85] as a Pennsylvania delegate put it, in order to gauge population densities throughout the state. After the first federal census, in 1790, they even had accurate population statistics to guide them. Crude though these methods were, they enabled legislators to approximate a state's then-current population center.

Legislators in most large states, then, fixed the state's current demographic center as the site for its new seat of government. In Pennsylvania, for example, delegates had placed the first new capital at Lancaster, near the state's then-current center of population. (See map 2.) But by 1810 the population had shifted and the capital was moved again. Legis-

[83]*Annals of Congress*, I: 846.
[84]*Charleston Morning Post*, March 15, 1786.
[85]*Poulson's American Daily Advertiser*, February 2, 1810.

lators deliberately rejected Bellafonte, a site close to the state's geographic center, in favor of Harrisburg, which seemed to be, in the representatives' words, "nearer the centre of population."[86] (See map 3.) In New York, legislators realized that their state's geographic center lay in Madison County, a region that was virtually uninhabited in 1797. As a result, they placed their new seat of government at Albany, located at the intersection of existing north-south and east-west settlement. (See map 2.) Virginia, North Carolina, and Georgia (in its first removal) also positioned their new seats of government at locations deemed to be the center of population. (See maps 1, 2, and 3.) Even the permanent national capital was placed near the country's demographic center of the time.[87]

Unlike legislators in the small states, politicians in the large states regarded population rather than territory as the most important variable affecting representation. In situating their capitals, they considered settlement patterns and population density rather than artificial lines on a map. The use of then-current population estimates helps explain what today appears to be the irrational placement of many seats of government in the original states. Though subject to change, a demographically central capital was more suitable for the larger states because it gave residents in all inhabited regions more equal access to—and presumably more equal representation in—the assembly. In contrast to their small-state neighbors, large-state legislators considered the state a demographic rather than a geographic unit.

The Limits of Removal

The era of removal came to an end in 1812. Among the original thirteen states, only Georgia would move its capital again, but it did so only after—and as a direct result of—the Civil War.[88] Other states would relocate their capitals from time to time, but never again was there a wave of removals all emanating from a common impulse. Americans had concluded that the physical relocation of capitals was not the

---

[86]*Journal of the First Session of the Ninth House of Representatives of Philadelphia—1798–1799* (Philadelphia, 1799), 127.

[87]For debates over the national capital, see, for example, *Annals of Congress*, I: 833–88, 1658–80. The first U.S. census, in 1790, showed that the nation's population center was located only twenty-three miles east of Baltimore, very close to the new U.S. capital, Washington, D.C. See Paullin, *Atlas of Historical Geography*, plate 80.

[88]In February 1869, a Georgia state constitutional convention voted to shift the capital from Milledgeville to Atlanta. See James C. Bonner, *Milledgeville: Georgia's Antebellum Capital* (Athens, Ga., 1978), 220.

best means to effect their end—the equalization of representation in the legislature.

In part, the removals ended because not one of the new capitals developed into a great metropolis the way Americans thought they would. Few, in fact, ever rose above the "degree of a village."[89] After the initial influx of people and businesses associated directly with the government, the new towns tended to stagnate. Sixteen years after the founding of Columbia, South Carolina, an observer noted that except during meetings of the assembly, "the town derives no particular advantage from being the seat of government."[90] An Annapolis resident attributed his town's failure to develop into a great commercial center to the very presence of government. The town's "being the residence of insolent great men," he said, "deterred many plain, independent, enterprising men from settling there."[91] The new national capital, Washington, D.C., remained for many decades nothing more than an "embryo capital."[92]

Not only did the new capitals fail to rival the colonial seats of government in population, prosperity, and grandeur, they barely sustained their own existence. In part, the egalitarianism of American society, one of the forces that compelled removal in the first place, inhibited the emergence of grand capitals. In Europe, the local gentry and aristocracy took up residence in the capitals. Their presence stimulated trade and created the demand for a wide variety of auxiliary goods and services. In the United States, no elite was capable of exerting such influence. Moreover, Americans established their capitals in places that had demonstrated no prior need for a large urban center. As modern central place theory shows, towns develop throughout the hinterland in accordance with the importance of the functions they provide to the surrounding areas.[93] Overestimating the attraction of government, Americans believed the very presence of the legislature and government admin-

[89]"Hillsborough Convention," August 4, 1788, in Clark, *State Records of North Carolina*, XXII: 34.

[90]François André Michaux, "Lowcountry and Upcountry South Carolina as Seen by a Famous Botanist, 1802–1803," in *South Carolina: The Grand Tour, 1780–1865*, ed. Thomas D. Clark (Columbia, S.C., 1973), 39–40.

[91]Hanson, *Considerations on Removal in Maryland*, 27.

[92]Quoted in James Sterling Young, *The Washington Community, 1800–1828* (New York, 1966), 41.

[93]Michael F. Dacey, "Analysis of Central Place and Point Patterns by a Nearest Neighbor Method," in *Proceedings of the IGU Symposium in Urban Geography, Lund 1960*, ed. Knut Norborg (Lund, Sweden, 1962), 55–60; Richard L. Morrill, "Simulation of Central Place Patterns over Time," in Norborg, *Proceedings of the IGU Symposium*, 109–11; James T. Lemon, "Urbanization and the Development of Eighteenth-Century Southeastern Pennsylvania and Adjacent Delaware," *William & Mary Quarterly*, 3d ser., 14 (1967), 50n.4.

istrative offices would generate wealth and stimulate population growth. Yet few scrambled to be near the seat of power.

Removal ended, however, for other reasons as well. In the process of moving their capitals, Americans had begun to reevaluate their ideas about representation. Before the Revolution, they had conceived of representation in strictly spatial terms. Equal representation meant spatial equality: ensuring that each community had equal access to the seat of government so that it could send representatives to meetings of the legislature, influence its proceedings, and supervise the legislators' actions.

The Revolution, however, had introduced another concept of equal representation. The emphasis on individual equality led to a demand for representation based on numbers rather than territory, on people rather than space.[94] In the same year that the removals began, citizens started experimenting with proportional representation. The first constitutions of Massachusetts, New York, and Pennsylvania included provisions that based representation in the lower houses of their legislatures on population. New Hampshire, Georgia, and South Carolina soon followed suit.[95] Yet many states resisted the new approach. By 1812, seven of the original thirteen states still had not reapportioned their assemblies.[96] Most of these other states had chosen the less radical alternative, trying to equalize representation in their assemblies by removing their state capitals.

Yet, time and time again, the removal question only led to the bigger question of apportionment in the legislature. In Pennsylvania, for example, westerners' demands for removal were consistently blocked by the same legislature in which the westerners were underrepresented. Only with the help of some disgruntled eastern delegates did westerners achieve victory in 1799; they could not have secured the bill's passage on their own.[97] The same was true in many other states. Remarking bitterly on the conflict in South Carolina, Robert Goodloe Harper said: "There can hardly be a question which will more deeply interest the upper country than the removal of the seat of government. But how was it carried: by their own strength? No, all their struggles for that purpose

---

[94]Pole, *Political Representation*, 198–204, 260–77, 314–38, 526–39.

[95]Ibid.; Willi Paul Adams, *The First American Constitutions: Republican Ideology and the Making of the State Constitutions in the Revolutionary Era* (Chapel Hill, N.C., 1980), 236–43.

[96]Rhode Island, Connecticut, Delaware, New Jersey, Maryland, North Carolina, and Virginia still had not adopted numerical representation for even the lower houses of their legislatures.

[97]*Kline's Weekly Carlisle Gazette* (Pennsylvania), May 1, 1799; *Bache's Philadelphia Aurora*, April 5, 1799.

were ineffectual 'till they were joined by some members from below."[98] Only when delegates from sections that were adequately represented came to their aid could supporters of removal succeed. On their own, they were essentially powerless.

More clearly than before, citizens began to understand the limitations of removal—that the real problem lay in the composition of the legislature, not in people's distance from it. Westerners saw that easterners, who had a disproportionately large share of representatives,[99] had no interest in their concerns. As citizens waged their battles, they realized that even if the capital were relocated and even if all sections sent their allotted number of delegates to the assembly, each area would still not be adequately represented. Only a comprehensive reapportionment of the legislature could achieve that goal.

Removal clarified the advantages of proportional representation as a means of equalizing representation. Citizens—and legislators responding to citizens' demands—became less wary of the method and more willing to experiment. As one spokesman put it, "A constitution should lay down some permanent ratio, by which the representation should afterwards encrease or decrease with the number of inhabitants."[100] Spatial equality was not enough.

Although settlement continued to expand westward, citizens in the thirteen original states no longer called for removal with the frequency or intensity that they once had. None of the original states, except Georgia, moved its capital again. Instead, from the 1820s through the 1840s, the states engaged in a new wave of constitution-writing, during which discussions about numerical representation dominated the proceedings. As a result, three more of the original states succeeded in converting to proportional representation. Most new states chose the method as well.[101] After 1812, the era of removal gave way to the age of reapportionment.

Beyond its impact on ideas of representation, removal had further

[98]Robert Goodloe Harper [Appius], *An Address to the People of South Carolina by the General Committee of the Representative Reform Association, at Columbia* (Charleston, S.C., 1794), 35.

[99]Lester J. Cappon et al., eds., *Atlas of Early American History: The Revolutionary Era, 1760–1790* (Princeton, N.J., 1976), 25, 62; Elisha P. Douglass, *Rebels and Democrats: The Struggle for Political Rights and Majority Rule during the American Revolution* (Chicago, 1955), 240–41; Pole, *Political Representation*, 172–78, 260–70, 314–38; Green, *Constitutional Development*, 168–70, 198–200.

[100]"Anonymous," "Four Letters on Interesting Subjects" (Philadelphia, 1776), in Hyneman and Lutz, *American Political Writings*, I: 387.

[101]Thorpe, *Federal and State Constitutions*, I: 536–48, 582–600; III: 1712–41; V: 2639–51; V: 2599–2614; V: 3104–17; VI: 3222–36; VII: 3819–28; Pole, *Political Representation*, 314–38; Gordon E. Baker, *The Reapportionment Revolution: Representation, Political Power, and the Supreme Court* (New York, 1967), 16–22.

consequences. Although participants had not explicitly identified themselves as members of small or large states, state size had played a determinative role in shaping legislators' choices of representative institutions. Whereas states with more territory had tended to place their capitals in their demographic centers, smaller states had positioned theirs relative to geographic factors. (See appendix 4.) Citizens in the large states were beginning to regard population as the most important variable in representation; those in the small states continued to believe that territory was the most crucial. Seemingly inconsequential at first, this split proved to be the harbinger of an increasingly important rift between the large states and the small states—a rift that would come to have an explosive meaning in the near future.

CHAPTER 2

Apportionment Divides
the States

As the implications of removal became apparent, the problem of representing extensive areas came to focus on the question of apportionment in the state legislatures. In extending republican government over large areas, Americans had to resolve the problem of if—and on what basis—representation should be given to outlying regions. Apportionment touched the very foundation of republicanism, as it determined the distribution of power within the legislature. In terms of its impact on subsequent legislation, no other decision had as far-reaching an impact.

As Americans began writing their state constitutions, they realized what some had already known: that the traditional methods of apportioning representatives on the basis of geographic units were unequal, unfair, and unrepublican. As a result, some states seized this opportunity to alter their apportionment systems in a fundamental fashion. They implemented a new means of distributing representatives, one in which representation was proportional to population. Yet other states chose to retain the traditional method of allocating representatives to counties, towns, and parishes, regardless of their populations.

These choices, however, did not occur randomly. In the quarter-century after the Revolution, state size proved to be a critical factor in determining which states kept corporate representation and which adopted proportional representation. As in the removal controversies, legislators discovered that states possessing widely divergent amounts of land and numbers of people had very different problems concerning representation. As they reviewed their methods of distributing representatives, the legislators in smaller states concluded that the traditional system, based on territory, was adequate for their needs, whereas the legislators in larger states believed that a newer method, based on population, should be adopted.

The Impetus for Innovation

As they came to America, the colonists drew on their English experience in devising methods of representation. In England, counties, boroughs, and universities had been the basis of representation. Each geographic unit was thought to comprise a community, and each community sent a designated number of delegates to the House of Commons.[1] Because representation was not based on population, vast inequities developed over time in the form of the so-called rotten boroughs. Old Sarum, for instance, had no human residents—only a few sheep— yet sent the same number of representatives to Parliament as Yorkshire, with nearly a million inhabitants.[2] By 1783, a Committee of the Commons reported that 1/170 of the population, or 11,075 voters, elected a majority of the delegates.[3] Nevertheless, the inequities continued to mount well into the nineteenth century.

In the seventeenth century, however, the deficiencies of territorial, or corporate, representation, as it was called, were not so obvious. In fact, the colonists apparently never considered using another method of apportionment. Drawing on their English background, all the colonies used some variation of the corporate system. New Englanders, for example, based representation on towns; the middle and southern colonists used counties; and South Carolinians adopted parishes as their basic unit of representation.[4] Before the Revolution, no American colony systematically based its representation on population.

The corporate method of representation presumed that physical proximity generated communal sentiment. Each geographic unit was

[1]A. L. Brown, "Parliament, c. 1377–1422," in *The English Parliament in the Middle Ages*, ed. R. G. Davies and J. H. Denton (Philadelphia, 1981), 118–19; J. R. Pole, *Political Representation in England and the Origins of the American Republic* (New York, 1966), 389; Robert MacKay, *Reapportionment: The Law and Politics* (New York, 1967), 29–30.

[2]Gordon E. Baker, *The Reapportionment Revolution: Representation, Political Power, and the Supreme Court* (New York, 1955), 15–16; MacKay, *Reapportionment*, 30; Pole, *Political Representation*, 396–97.

[3]*The State of the Representation of England and Wales, Delivered to the Society, of the Friends of the People, Associated for the Purpose of obtaining a Parliamentary Reform, on Saturday the 9th of February 1793* (London, 1793), 5.

[4]J. R. Pole, *The Seventeenth Century: The Sources of Legislative Power* (Charlottesville, Va., 1969), 64–65; Michael Kammen, *Deputyes and Libertyes: The Origins of Representative Government in Colonial America* (New York, 1969), 13–68.

thought to be an organic, cohesive community, whose residents knew one another, held common values, and shared compatible economic interests. The smaller the community, the more likely that its citizens would identify with one another. In 1796, for example, geographer Jedidiah Morse described Connecticut as "the most populous [state], in proportion to its extent. . . . A traveller in any of these roads, even in the most unsettled parts of the state, will seldom pass more than two or three miles without finding a house or cottage, and a farm. . . . The whole state resembles a well cultivated garden."[5] Large distances, in contrast, bred a diversity of peoples and values.[6] Although actual settlements were never as unified in practice as in theory, the idea contained some truth. Sharing a common history and future reinforced the sense of communal identity among inhabitants.[7]

Corporate representation also implied that equal representation meant the equal representation of communities, not individuals. "This State," commented some citizens from Massachusetts, "is Constituted of a great number of Distinct and very unequal Corporations which Corporations are the Immediate Constituant part of the State and Individuals are only the Remote parts."[8] Since each community was believed to speak with a single voice, vast disparities in population among the communities were not thought to matter for representation purposes. As long as each community received some representation in the legislature, all citizens were considered adequately represented. As a critic of territorial representation put it, "Hitherto the people of New-Jersey have not been represented in the legislature, according to their *constituent* capacity, but according to certain *geographical* descriptions: the *counties* have been represented by *equal* delegations, without regard to the comparative state of population and property."[9] The colony, and later the

[5]Jedidiah Morse, *The American Universal Geography, or a View of the Present State of All the Empires, Kingdoms, States, and Republics in the Known World, and of the United States of America in Particular* (Boston, 1796), pt. 1: 453.

[6]See, for example, Elijah Parish, *A New System of Modern Geography* (Newburyport, Mass., 1810), 116.

[7]See the various community studies that suggest the existence of communal feeling, even in the South, where settlement was more dispersed—for example, Kenneth A. Lockridge, *A New England Town: The First Hundred Years* (New York, 1970); Philip Greven, Jr., *Population, Land, and Family in Colonial Andover, Massachusetts* (Ithaca, 1970); Rhys Isaac, *The Transformation of Virginia, 1740–1790* (Chapel Hill, N.C., 1982); Kevin P. Kelly, " 'In Dispers'd Plantations': Settlement Patterns in Seventeenth-Century Surry County, Virginia," in *The Chesapeake in the Seventeenth Century: Essays on Anglo-American Society and Politics*, ed. Thad W. Tate and David L. Ammerman (New York, 1979), 202–5.

[8]Statement from Lincoln (Middlesex County), May 22, 1780, in *The Popular Sources of Political Authority: Documents on the Massachusetts Constitution of 1780*, ed. Oscar Handlin and Mary Handlin (Cambridge, Mass., 1966), 663.

[9]William Griffith, *Eumenes: Being a Collection of Papers, Written for the Purpose of Exhibiting Some of the More Prominent Errors and Omissions of the Constitution of New Jersey* (Trenton, N.J., 1799), 53.

state, was the sum of its constituent communities, achieving a grand harmony among its parts through the mechanism of the legislature.

When the Revolution compelled Americans to express their ideas about representation, they articulated the concept known as actual representation. In this view, the representative assembly was regarded as a substitute for the electors' actual participation in the law-making process. The legislature, according to John Adams, should be "in miniature an exact portrait of the people at large. It should think, feel, reason, and act like them."[10] If three-fourths of the people opposed a bill, the legislature should oppose it in the same proportion. The assembly should act, said Thomas Paine, "in the same manner as the whole body would act were they present."[11] In a very real sense, the legislature's laws were the people's laws.

A commitment to actual representation led Americans to see a contradiction between ideals and realities in their own state legislatures. Actual representation implied that each individual should be equally represented in the assembly. Every elector's vote should be worth as much as every other elector's vote. Corporate apportionment, on the other hand, promoted equality among communities rather than individuals. Under the system, a minority of the people might actually elect a majority of the representatives. In his *Notes on the State of Virginia*, for example, Thomas Jefferson pointed out that a small number of people living in the Tidewater elected over half the delegates in both houses of Virginia's legislature. "These nineteen thousand [electors]," he said, "living in one part of the country, give law to upwards of thirty thousand living in another."[12] Under territorial apportionment, in other words, the majority did not necessarily rule.

Another alternative existed, however. Numerical apportionment, or proportional representation, as it was called, could resolve this contradiction as well as guarantee majority rule. This method established a ratio of representatives to people—for example, one delegate for every fifty thousand citizens. Districts could be drawn to encompass a certain number of people—and the boundaries redrawn as the population increased or decreased. As the author of the "Essex Result" put it in 1778, "If in adjusting the representation of freemen, any ten are reduced into one, all the other tens should be alike reduced: or if any hundred should be reduced to one, all the other hundreds should have the same reduc-

---

[10]John Adams, "Thoughts on Government" (1776), in *The Works of John Adams*, ed. Charles Francis Adams (Boston, 1851), IV: 195.

[11]Thomas Paine, "Common Sense," in *Tracts of the American Revolution*, ed. Merrill Jensen (Indianapolis, 1967; orig. publ. 1776), 404.

[12]Thomas Jefferson, *Notes on the State of Virginia* (New York, 1964; orig. publ. 1794), 112–13.

tion."[13] Under this system, the majority of people would always receive the majority of representatives.

Revolutionary ideology, with its emphasis on natural rights and individual equality, gave impetus to the drive for proportional representation. The Pennsylvania constitution of 1776, for example, stated, "Representation in proportion to the number of taxable inhabitants is the only principle which can at all times secure liberty, and make the voice of a majority of the people the law of the land."[14] In 1794 Robert Goodloe Harper of South Carolina observed, "A representative government cannot be free, unless it be so constituted, that each member of the community may possess, by his representative, the same portion of power, in public affairs, that he would have been entitled to himself, had government been administered by all the people in person. . . . All, therefore, should be equal by representation."[15] Numerical apportionment would be the means of achieving majority rule.

When the Continental Congress urged the colonists to form their own governments in May of 1776, it provided the perfect opportunity for Americans to eliminate inequities produced by corporate representation. Yet some states chose not to take this course. In fact, in the formative period for representative institutions, from 1776 to 1812, less than half of the original thirteen states chose to reapportion their legislatures on the basis of population. This fact does not suggest that people in some states were more principled than those in other states; rather, it indicates that factors other than revolutionary fervor were at work.

In the quarter-century after the Revolution, state size became one of the most important factors determining whether or not citizens in a particular state would adopt numerical representation in the lower house

[13]"Theophilus Parsons," "Essex Result" (Newburyport, Mass., 1778), in *American Political Writing during the Founding Era, 1760–1805,* ed. Charles S. Hyneman and Donald S. Lutz (Indianapolis, 1983), I: 497. I am using *numerical representation* as a synonym for *proportional representation,* the term used at the time. In the late nineteenth century, proportional representation took on another meaning—a system in which political parties received representation in proportion to the votes they received. It did not have this meaning in the late eighteenth century.

[14]Francis N. Thorpe, comp., *The Federal and State Constitutions, Colonial Charters, and Other Organic Laws of the States, Territories, and Colonies Now or Heretofore Forming the United States of America* (Washington, D.C., 1909), V: 3086. For good discussions in the secondary literature of the development of numerical apportionment in the states, see Pole, *Political Representation,* 172–89, 262–65, 274–76, 315–21, 535–36; Elisha P. Douglass, *Rebels and Democrats: The Struggle for Political Rights and Majority Rule during the American Revolution* (Chicago, 1955), 33–34, 43–44, 165–66; Gordon S. Wood, *Creation of the American Republic, 1776–1787* (New York, 1969), 162–73; Willi Paul Adams, *The First American Constitutions: Republican Ideology and the Making of the State Constitutions of the Revolutionary Era* (Chapel Hill, N.C., 1980), esp. 233–43.

[15]Robert Goodloe Harper [Appius], *An Address to the People of South Carolina by the General Committee of the Representative Reform Association, at Columbia* (Charleston, S.C., 1794), 4–5.

of their state assembly. As they debated the structure of representation for their states, citizens in the larger states faced representation problems that were fundamentally different from those in the smaller states. As a result, they selected different methods of apportioning representatives for their legislatures. Citizens in the smaller states usually kept the traditional territorial method; those in the larger states experimented with the more innovative numerical approach. It was not that states deliberately coordinated their choices with those of states of comparable size. Rather, the delegates of each state came to their own conclusions independently of one another. Common underlying factors in states of similar size helped lead the legislators to similar conclusions.

Representatives in most of the smaller states concluded that corporate representation was adequate for their needs. In Rhode Island the old charter was reaffirmed. Although the four original towns received extra representation, each of the other towns received two seats in the lower house of the assembly.[16] In Connecticut, which kept its original charter, each town was to elect two representatives to the assembly.[17] In New Jersey and Delaware, each county sent three delegates to the lower houses of their legislatures.[18] Maryland's counties were allotted four members each.[19] Among states having smaller areas and populations, only New Hampshire abandoned corporate representation.[20] Having made their choice, most of the smaller states continued to use the territorial method well into the nineteenth century.[21]

In larger states, legislators tended to implement proportional representation in the lower houses of their legislatures. Pennsylvanians, for example, accepted a system of numerical apportionment in their first constitution of 1776 and reaffirmed the principle in their 1790 constitution.[22] New Yorkers adopted this method for their lower house in 1777.[23] In 1780 Massachusetts, which at that time included Maine, retained the town as its basic unit of apportionment but granted additional representation to towns with larger populations.[24] When Georgians rewrote their state constitution in 1789, they proportioned representation to population in their lower house.[25] Although South Carolin-

[16]Thorpe, *Constitutions*, VI: 3211–22.
[17]Ibid., I: 529–46.
[18]Ibid., I: 562–68; V: 2594–98.
[19]Ibid., III: 1686–1701.
[20]Ibid., IV: 2451–90.
[21]Ibid., I: 536–48; III: 1712–41; V: 2639–51; V: 2599–2614; V: 3104–17; VI: 3222–36; VII: 3819–28.
[22]Ibid., V: 3081–3103.
[23]Ibid., V: 2623–38.
[24]Ibid., III: 1888–1923.
[25]Ibid., II: 777–802.

ians accepted the principle of numerical apportionment as early as 1778, the state did not actually implement the system until 1808.[26] Among the states with large western territories, only Virginia and North Carolina refused to adopt numerical apportionment during the quarter-century after the Revolution.[27]

To be sure, not all these states adopted the same system of numerical apportionment. Wide differences existed, for example, in the represented populations—that is, in the number of inhabitants counted for the purpose of determining representation. New York, for example, defined its represented population rather narrowly, including only the electors in each county—which meant, essentially, the qualified white males who had reached their majority.[28] Pennsylvania and Massachusetts chose a somewhat less restrictive basis, counting all "taxable inhabitants" or "rateable polls."[29] Any individual who was taxed, whether man, woman, freed person, or slave, was thus included in the represented population. Georgia's 1798 constitution contained among the most liberal provisions of any state. Imitating the federal Constitution, it based representation on each county's "respective numbers of free white persons, and including three-fifths of all the people of color."[30] None of the original thirteen state constitutions, however, made total population, including women, children, and blacks, its basis of apportionment.

Equal Representation and State Size

In theory, corporate representation could have been extended to states of any size. In practice, however, the system's limitations and inequities became most problematic in the states with the most territory. As a result, the larger states were more willing than the smaller states to abandon the traditional method.

First, in order for territorial representation to work, the legislature had to be consistently willing to create new political units—and to grant these units the full benefits of representation in the assembly. Even in colonial times, extending representation to newly settled areas had been one of the most difficult problems governments faced. Battles often raged between the governor and the legislature over which branch had

[26]Ibid., VI: 3241–67.
[27]Ibid., V: 2787–94; VII: 3812–19.
[28]Ibid., V: 2629–30.
[29]Ibid., III: 1898; V: 3086, 3093.
[30]Ibid., II: 791–92.

the authority to grant additional representation. In the charter colonies, the legislatures claimed an exclusive right over this power. In the royal colonies, however, control shifted between the assemblies and the royal governors—although the legislatures often had the upper hand.[31] In 1767 British officials prohibited the legislatures from enacting any further laws altering or regulating the composition of the assemblies.[32] All sides realized that the power to grant additional representation could significantly alter the legislature's character.

During the colonial period, the method of extending representation varied widely from colony to colony. When a newly settled region became sufficiently populous, the legislature usually received petitions from citizens requesting the creation of a new county, town, or parish. If it chose to act on the petition, it would either create a new political unit or divide an existing community into smaller units. Some colonies regularly granted representation to newly settled areas. Virginia, for example, created an average of five new counties in every decade from 1700 to 1767 and always allowed each new county to send two delegates to the House of Burgesses—the same number that the older counties sent.[33] Similarly, newly incorporated towns in Connecticut received the same number of representatives as the more established towns.[34]

Yet legislators saw that granting equal representation to newly created communities meant diminishing their own power. To preserve their superiority, some legislatures withheld representation completely or assigned new regions fewer representatives than the older areas had. In the early eighteenth century, for example, Massachusetts stopped giving representation to newly established towns, most of which were in the interior.[35] As a result, westerners had little say in the colony's government. The Pennsylvania assembly, too, consistently gave its backcountry counties fewer representatives than counties along the seacoast.[36] By 1775 Pennsylvania's three eastern counties had twenty-six delegates whereas the eight western counties, with over half the population, had only fifteen delegates.[37] In North Carolina, Governor George

[31]Jack P. Greene, *The Quest for Power: The Lower Houses of the Assembly in the Southern Royal Colonies, 1689–1776* (Chapel Hill, N.C., 1963), 171–85; Pole, *Political Representation*, 54–75, 260–70.

[32]Greene, *Quest for Power*, 185; Raymond C. Bailey, *Popular Influence upon Public Policy: Petitioning in Eighteenth-Century Virginia*, Contributions in Legal Studies No. 10 (Westport, Conn., 1979), 71.

[33]Bailey, *Popular Influence*, 72–73.

[34]Richard L. Bushman, *From Puritan to Yankee: Character and the Social Order in Connecticut, 1690–1765* (New York, 1967), 249–50.

[35]Pole, *Political Representation*, 63–64, 173–74.

[36]Ibid., 110, 262–64.

[37]Merrill Jensen, ed., *The Documentary History of the Ratification of the Constitution*, Vol. II: Pennsylvania (Madison, Wis., 1976), 30.

Burrington commented in 1731 on the inequities of that colony's system, noting that "a Small part of the Province have Twenty Six Representatives [and] all the Remainder but ten."[38] Assessing the situation, one North Carolinian remarked, "Men, who have more than a proper degree of power, are seldom known to surrender it freely."[39]

Because of the greater opportunity for settlement, states with western lands had more opportunities to withhold representation than states having little territory. Furthermore, large states often had an entrenched elite unwilling to share power with the upstart westerners. By the time of the Revolution, the problem of underrepresentation was reaching crisis proportions.[40] (See map 5.)

Large states were also less likely than small states to create the kind of electoral units necessary to foster equality. In order for corporate representation to be equitable, a particular set of conditions had to be fulfilled. Geographic units needed to be made nearly equal in area, and population had to be evenly distributed throughout the state. Under these circumstances, all the political units would contain roughly comparable numbers of people. Even though each unit might receive the same number of representatives, a de facto equality would prevail.

These conditions were more likely to pertain in the small states than the large. States with vast landholdings usually had a great deal of variation in the size of their political units. Newly created frontier districts tended to encompass much greater territory than the older, more established eastern districts. Similarly, population distribution varied more widely. In large states, the population density varied immensely from place to place. Population tended to be most heavily concentrated along the coast, with less dense settlement farther inland. Clusters of population appeared throughout the state at locations favorable for cultivation and commerce. Yet large regions remained unsettled, at least by whites. Smaller states, in contrast, had no frontier, and such vast disparities were uncommon. Geographic units tended to be more equal in area and population more compactly and evenly distributed. (See maps 1, 2, and 3.)

Greater variation in the size of geographic units and population densities throughout the state led to greater inequities in representation under corporate representation. If each unit received the same number of representatives regardless of its population, some communities were

[38]Quoted in Greene, *Quest for Power*, 175–76.

[39]Hugh Williamson, *The History of North Carolina* (Philadelphia, 1812), II: 57–59.

[40]The desire to secede and form a new state was an extreme consequence of such underrepresentation. See Peter S. Onuf, *The Origins of the Federal Republic: Jurisdictional Controversies in the United States, 1775–1787* (Philadelphia, 1983), 34–40.

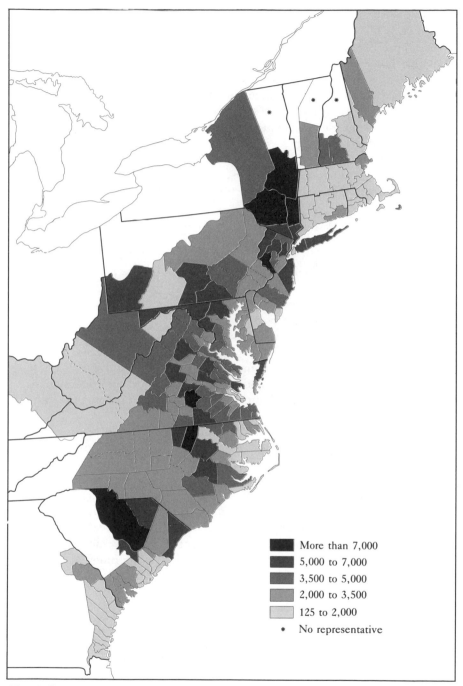

More than 7,000
5,000 to 7,000
3,500 to 5,000
2,000 to 3,500
125 to 2,000
* No representative

Map 5. Ratio of population to representatives in the lower houses of the colonial assemblies, per county/parish, c. 1775

SOURCE: Lester J. Cappon et al., eds., *Atlas of Early American History: The Revolutionary Era, 1760–1790* (Princeton, N.J., 1976), 25.

overrepresented and others were underrepresented relative to the state's norm. For example, if each county elected two delegates, a person's vote in a county of one thousand was worth much more than in a county of twenty thousand.[41] Individuals in counties with fewer people were more likely to know their representatives personally and to have greater influence on the election's outcome than those living in larger counties. Because these circumstances were more likely to emerge in states having a great deal of territory than in those with little territory, corporate apportionment produced the greatest disparities in representation within the larger states. (See maps 5 and 6.)

South Carolina: The Trade-off That Failed

A detailed examination of the apportionment debate in one large and one small state suggests why state size proved to be such a compelling force in apportionment decisions. South Carolina provides a good example of the controversy in a large state. Although it took longer for the state to institute proportional representation than in many of the other large states, this fact resulted in an extensive written record on the subject. Moreover, South Carolina offers a fascinating example of a state that was willing to accept the principle of numerical representation as early as 1778 but that delayed implementing the fact for more than thirty years.

In the colonial era, South Carolinians had developed a system of apportionment that favored those who already held power in the legislature. Representation was based on the parish. Legislators had the authority to assign as many or as few representatives to each parish as they saw fit. Because there was no established formula according to which they distributed representatives, the number of representatives given to a particular parish bore no discernible relationship to its wealth, population, or territory. As one contemporary put it, the assembly gave "a definite number of representatives . . . to definite portions of territory . . . without the guidance of any fixed principle."[42] The only consid-

[41]As William Griffith of New Jersey observed, "Surely if a law were proposed, and the sense of the *people* actually taken in *person*, and not by delegation, it would be thought monstrous, that two hundred votes from Hunterdon [county] (for instance) should be balanced by one hundred from Burlington [county]." Griffith, *Eumenes*, 53.

[42]David Ramsay, *History of South-Carolina, from Its First Settlement in 1670 to the Year 1808* (Newberry, S.C., 1858; orig. publ. 1808), II: 246. For a discussion of the development of numerical representation in the large states of Virginia, Pennsylvania, and Massachusetts, see Pole, *Political Representation*.

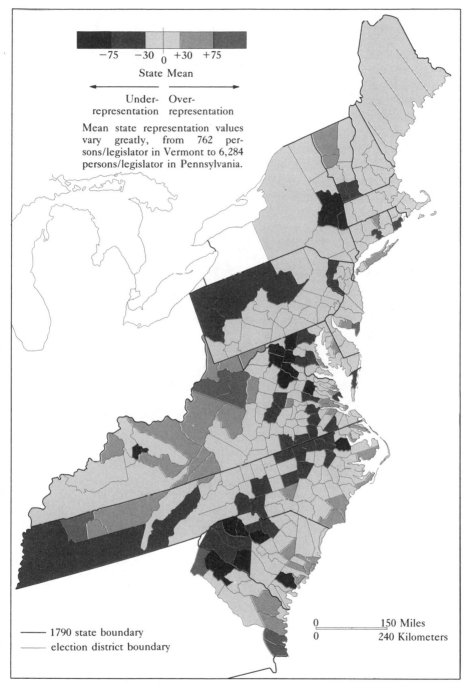

State Mean

Under- Over-
representation representation

Mean state representation values
vary greatly, from 762 per-
sons/legislator in Vermont to 6,284
persons/legislator in Pennsylvania.

−75   −30   0   +30   +75

0   150 Miles
0   240 Kilometers

—— 1790 state boundary
—— election district boundary

Map 6. Over- and underrepresentation in the lower houses of the state legislatures,
percent deviation of county/parish mean representation from the state mean, c. 1790

SOURCE: Lester J. Cappon et al., eds., *Atlas of Early American History: The Revolutionary Era, 1760–
1790* (Princeton, N.J., 1976), 62.

eration seemed to be that easterners from the state's low-country wanted to maintain their numerical superiority in the assembly.

As more people moved into the state's western regions, discontent with the system increased. Some areas were underrepresented; others had no representation at all. Yet, when they wrote their first state constitution, low-country delegates, who dominated the assembly, turned a deaf ear to the up-country's pleas. Written by the legislature, the 1776 constitution merely perpetuated the traditional pattern of arbitrary apportionment.[43] A South Carolina legislator observed that members had been distributed "entirely at random. No census of the people was taken, no estimate of the relative wealth of the different election districts, no survey of their territorial extent. This *accident*," he said, "gave a vast and most injurious preponderance to certain parts of the country."[44]

Up-country representatives from the west continued their protests. At this time, easterners had only one-fifth of the state's population but more than twice as many representatives as westerners.[45] In 1778, the legislature appeared to relent, rewriting the constitution and incorporating ostensibly significant changes in apportionment. The new plan, which was to go into effect in seven years, based representation in the lower house on a combination of taxable property and white population. A periodic census would be taken to keep representation commensurate with population.[46]

The easterners, who were supposed to relinquish their power gradually, did not keep their word. In 1785, the legislature was supposed to order a census and reapportion the assembly in accordance with it. But nothing happened. The legislature simply ignored the constitution. The delegates created two new western counties but left the previous system intact.[47] In 1786, Judge Pendleton proposed a bill to revise apportionment in the manner prescribed by the constitution. "Since the time of framing our constitution," he noted, "great alterations had taken place in this state—both in regard to actual property, and the number of inhabitants—the districts of Camden and Ninety-Six in particular had become far more populous . . . and yet their representation is still the

[43]Thorpe, *Constitutions*, VI: 3245.

[44]Joseph Alston, *Speech of Joseph Alston, Member of the House of Representatives for Winyaw, in a Committee of the Whole . . .* (Georgetown, S.C., 1808), 21, 23.

[45]Fletcher M. Green, *Constitutional Development in the South Atlantic States, 1776–1860* (Chapel Hill, N.C., 1930), 115.

[46]Thorpe, *Constitutions*, VI: 3251–52.

[47]Green, *Constitutional Development*, 119; William A. Schaper, "Sectionalism and Representation in South Carolina," in *Annual Report of the American Historical Association for the Year 1900* (Washington, D.C., 1901), 369; Alston, *Speech*, 23.

same."[48] Although the House agreed to establish a committee to examine the matter, no further action was taken.

The low-country delegates were in a quandary. As the number of westerners increased, so did their demands for reapportionment. Perhaps in an effort to divert attention from the apportionment question, low-country legislators devised a compromise. In return for the westerners' acceptance of the status quo on representation, they agreed to pass a bill in 1786 moving the seat of government from Charleston to Columbia.[49] A delegate from the low-country explained the transaction as a mutually beneficial exchange between east and west. According to South Carolinian Henry De Sassure, the westerners obtained the capital "by the aid of some of the lower members, who conceived the change just (though inconvenient to them) from the old spot, where it had remained a century, and which was dear to the whole lower country, to the very place designated by the leaders of the opposite party. This change was made entirely against the interests, and chiefly at the expense of the sea coast."[50] De Sassure explained that the up-country, in gratitude, should relinquish its claims to greater representation in the legislature.[51] The exchange was, after all, a trade-off between forms of representation; the westerners received greater proximity to the capital, which would ensure better attendance by their representatives, in return for dropping their demands for more representatives.

The easterners clearly hoped that removal would placate the westerners and quiet discontent in the region. Pendleton remarked that moving the capital would "mitigate difficulties experienced in the administration of government, by those who were situated in different parts of the state" and "conciliate the affections of the people."[52] Speaking more naively than realistically, historian David Ramsay commented in 1808: "Since removal, party division between the upper and lower country had diminished. The inhabitants of both, by being better acquainted, are become more like one people; and entertain fewer jealousies or prejudices against each other."[53]

[48]*Charleston Morning Post & Daily Advertiser* (South Carolina), February 4, 1786. See also *State Gazette of South-Carolina* (Charleston), February 6, 1786.

[49]Lark Emerson Adams, ed., *Journals of the House of Representatives, 1785–1786* (Columbia, S.C., 1979), 573, 596; *Acts, Ordinances, and Resolves of the General Assembly of the State of South-Carolina, Passed in March, 1786* (Charleston, 1786), 56–58.

[50]Henry W. De Sassure [Phocion], *Letters on the Questions of the Justice and Expediency of Going into Alterations of the Representation in the Legislature of South Carolina, as Fixed by the Constitution* (Charleston, S.C., 1795), 25.

[51]Ibid., 23–27.

[52]*Charleston Morning Post & Daily Advertiser*, March 3, 1786.

[53]Ramsay, *History of South-Carolina*, II: 241.

The westerners, however, were not soothed by mere removal and soon openly violated the terms of the compromise. They continued to agitate for a change in the basis of representation as well as a comprehensive reapportionment of the legislature. Attacking the existing constitution, one South Carolinian claimed in 1789 that the current method of apportionment "establishe[d] a representation of the people upon unequal, i.e., unjust principles."[54]

In 1790, the people—not the legislators—gathered to write a new state constitution. Apportionment was a major concern. Yet those supporting substantial reforms soon realized that they could not make any significant progress because apportionment for the convention had been done by the same inequitable process as for the assembly. Robert Goodloe Harper despaired, "No reform, however desirable to four fifths of the people, could be made without the low country's consent."[55] The westerners, as a result, were unable to pass their proposed changes.

The convention moved on to other considerations. Delegates voted to reduce the size of the lower house and increase the size of the upper, a change that gave the westerners slightly more representatives than they had had but still far fewer than they deserved according to their strength in numbers.[56] Soon after, the eastern delegates attempted to reverse the west's victory in regard to the capital. Believing that the up-country had reneged on its half of the bargain, they wanted to return the capital to its eastern location. After a heated debate, a motion to return the capital to Charleston lost by only one vote. A similar resolution as to whether Columbia should be the state's permanent seat of government won by only four votes.[57]

Low-country members, however, kept at it. They eventually succeeded in passing an amendment that essentially created a system of dual capitals. The state was to support public offices for the surveyor-general and secretary of state in both Charleston and Columbia. The court of appeals would hold sessions in both towns. The governor, moreover, was required to reside in Columbia only when the legislature was in session.[58] Columbia was now the capital in name only. Although low-

[54]*The Carlisle Gazette & the Western Repository of Knowledge* (Pennsylvania), August 26, 1789.

[55]Harper, *Address to South Carolina*, 28. See also Green, *Constitutional Development*, 121.

[56]Green, *Constitutional Development*, 121–22; Schaper, "Sectionalism and Representation," 378–79; Jerome J. Nadelhaft, "'The Snarls of Invidious Animals': The Democratization of Revolutionary South Carolina," in *Sovereign States in an Age of Uncertainty*, ed. Ronald Hoffman and Peter J. Albert (Charlottesville, Va., 1981), 91.

[57]David Duncan Wallace, *South Carolina: A Short History, 1520–1948* (Columbia, S.C., 1961), 342–43; Schaper, "Sectionalism and Representation," 376–77.

[58]Thorpe, *Constitutions*, VI: 3260, 3265; Yates Snowden, ed., *History of South Carolina* (Chicago, 1920), 512–13.

country delegates had not actually succeeded in returning the seat of government to Charleston, they had been able to strip the western capital of its power and significance.

Once the compromise broke down, a war of words broke out over the merits of numerical representation. Writing under the pseudonym "Appius," Robert Goodloe Harper spoke on behalf of the up-country. Henry W. De Sassure, under the name "Phocion," and Timothy Ford, under the guise "Americanus," supported the low-country position.[59] Discussions centered on the possibility of implementing numerical apportionment in a state so large and with such deep-rooted geographical divisions. The easterners believed that the westerners' values and economic interests were hostile to their own; the westerners claimed proportional representation as their right.

The division went deeper. As in other southern states, the inhabitants of eastern areas tended to cultivate labor-intensive crops, such as rice, cotton, and indigo. This region was one of large plantations and huge slave populations. Settlers of the up-country tended to have smaller farms, where they grew wheat or corn and raised livestock. Although some back-country farmers did own slaves, their holdings tended to be much smaller. Moreover, slaves constituted a far smaller proportion of the total population than in the eastern regions.[60] "The upper and lower countries have opposite habits and views in almost every particular," observed Harper in 1794. "One is accustomed to expense," he said, "the other to frugality. . . . One imports almost every article of consumption, and pays for it in produce; the other is far removed from navigation, has very little to export, and must therefore supply its own wants. . . . One wishes for slaves, the other will be better off without them."[61] Low-countrymen viewed westerners as "strangers to our interests, our customs & our concerns."[62] Although inhabitants of the same state, residents of the two regions felt little sense of kinship with one another.

Low-country representatives contended that the current system of apportionment was appropriate under existing conditions and should not be changed. Representation, they said, should be related to taxation, to a section's wealth and ability to support the government. Because the

[59]Harper, *Address to South Carolina*; De Sassure, *Letters on Justice and Expediency*; Timothy Ford [Americanus], *The Constitutionalist: Or, an Enquiry How Far It Is Expedient and Proper to Alter the Constitution of South-Carolina* (Charleston, S.C., 1794).

[60]Jedidiah Morse, *The American Geography: or, A View of the Present Situation of the United States of America* (London, 1792), 251, 378, 395–96, 413–14, 417–18, 424–25, 428–30, 432–33, 445–48.

[61]Harper, *Address to South Carolina*, 31.

[62]Ford, *Constitutionalist*, 25.

easterners paid the greatest proportion of taxes, they believed they were entitled to a preponderance of representatives. De Sassure noted, "As a state divided into two great and distinct countries remarkably distinguished, the one for its possession of great wealth, or the means of public contribution; the other for its superior population; . . . there is a peculiar propriety in the state of South-Carolina adhering to the system of representation found on the combinations of population and property."[63] He warned that if the westerners were given representation in proportion to their numbers, they would use their power to oppress the east. They might place onerous taxes on slaves or on large estates—or, worse yet, free the slaves altogether.[64]

Proportional representation could work, De Sassure maintained, only "if the population of the several counties and parishes was nearly equal, and the property liable to bear the public burthens was pretty equally distributed throughout the counties and parishes. . . . Then the claim to a representation on the principle of population alone would be in some measure reasonable, because there would be no danger of oppression over any part of the state."[65] Until that time, the westerners should neither ask nor expect the easterners to relinquish their hold on the legislature. As Timothy Ford commented, "Though we take you into our association, content that you should share the government, yet we can never surrender ourselves into your hands with power to dispose of us as you please."[66] As a small and ever-shrinking proportion of the population, the easterners had to launch a frontal assault on the principle of proportional representation in order to defend the status quo.

Yet the easterners' resistance failed to stifle the westerners' support of the principle. Over time, the disparity between the westerners' strength in numbers and lack of strength in the legislature grew increasingly evident. Harper observed that the easterners "saw this inequality, already so enormous, becoming daily greater and more formidable, by the rapid increase of population and wealth in the upper districts."[67] In 1802, a House committee resolved that "the apportionment of representatives of the people of this state, in the legislature thereof, is partial and unequal, . . . a bill ought to be brought in to carry the spirit of the above resolution into complete effect."[68] Yet although the spirit was willing, the legislature once again did nothing.

Not until 1808 did the legislature finally capitulate. In that year,

[63]De Sassure, *Letters on Justice and Expediency*, 6.
[64]Ibid., 19.
[65]Ibid., 14.
[66]Ford, *Constitutionalist*, 25.
[67]Harper, *Address to South Carolina*, iv.
[68]*Carolina Gazette* (Charleston, S.C.), December 23, 1802.

Joseph Alston, a House member from Winyaw parish, gave an impassioned speech in a Committee of the Whole in which he traced the rocky course of reapportionment in South Carolina since the Revolution. "For fourteen years," he declaimed, "the present question has agitated the minds of our countrymen; for fourteen years the voice of complaint, and supplication for relief, has been raised; but, like the voice of the unhappy victim of the storm, cast upon some lonely and desert coast, it has been raised in vain."[69] He scrutinized the present system, pointing out the inequities. Not only did it give one geographic region an unfair advantage over the other, but it also violated the principle of majority rule. "Nothing is more clear," he said, "than that a great majority of the people have had no voice, have never had the slightest agency in what is, nevertheless, pretended to be their own [government]."[70] He argued that a constitutional convention should be called specifically for the purpose of reforming the state's apportionment procedures and insisted that more delays were unjust as well as untenable in the current political climate.[71]

Surprisingly enough, such an amendment did pass later that year. The new arrangement provided a formula for apportioning representatives in the lower house, based on a combination of the number of white inhabitants and the taxes paid by each district. A decennial census would keep representation proportional to population. To avoid a repetition of the legislature's previous failure to abide by the constitution, a clause was added: "If the enumeration herein directed should not be made in the course of the year appointed for the purpose by these amendments, it shall be the duty of the governor to have it effected as soon thereafter as shall be practicable."[72]

After thirty years, the up-country had finally succeeded in establishing an explicit formula for distributing representatives. Although this formula took wealth as well as population into consideration, it recognized the principle of numerical representation. Moreover, South Carolinians could now have some confidence that this reform would actually be put into effect.

New Jersey's Struggle over Corporate Representation

In terms of the debate in a small state, New Jersey offers a good example, although not because it was typical. In fact, the state experi-

[69]Alston, *Speech*, 19.
[70]Ibid., 23.
[71]Ibid., 27.
[72]Thorpe, *Constitutions*, VI: 3266.

enced much more controversy over apportionment than did the other small states. For this reason, however, New Jersey participants left a more explicit record on the subject than did participants in the other small states. Yet, like the other small states, New Jersey chose to retain corporate representation until the mid-nineteenth century.

Although relatively small in area, New Jersey was deeply divided— even before the apportionment question arose. The state was split into two distinct geographic and cultural regions. West Jersey was wealthier, it was dominated by Quakers, and it looked to Philadelphia for its cultural guidance. East Jersey was populated by farmers, who, if not debt-ridden, tended to be of modest means; they looked to New York for cultural and economic direction.[73] As in the larger states, each section battled for control of the legislature. Apportionment represented an important weapon in this battle.

Under the state's first constitution, written in 1776, each county sent three representatives to the legislature's lower house. Although the consitution retained territorial representation, it did include a provision offering the possibility for a future reapportionment. According to the constitution, "If a majority of representatives . . . shall . . . judge it equitable and proper, to add to or diminish the number or proportion of the members of Assembly for any county or counties in this Colony, then, and in such case, the same may, on the principles of more equal representation, be lawfully done."[74] Yet even though New Jersey residents recognized the existence of other methods of apportionment, they remained committed to the territorial system.

For some years thereafter, East and West Jersey coexisted in relative peace. Because there were seven western counties and six eastern ones, neither side had an overwhelming majority in the legislature. Nevertheless, by the 1790s, discontent with the powerful West Jersey "Junto," consisting of members from the southern part of the state, mounted.[75] Believing they had something to gain, the easterners wanted the legislature to act on the constitution's "equal representation" clause. In 1797, the assembly finally did act, passing a law to increase representation in three of the state's more populous counties—Hunterdon, Burlington, and Sussex—and to reduce it in Cumberland and Cape May

[73]David Hawke, *The Colonial Experience* (Indianapolis, 1966), 225–29, 479–80; Richard P. McCormick, *Experiment in Independence: New Jersey in the Critical Period, 1781–1789* (New Brunswick, N.J., 1950), viii, 43–44; Thomas J. Fleming, *New Jersey: A Bicentennial History* (New York, 1977), 87.

[74]Thorpe, *Constitutions*, V: 2595; William C. Wright, *The Development of the New Jersey Legislature from Colonial Times to the Present* (Trenton, N.J., 1976), 33.

[75]Alan Shank, *New Jersey Reapportionment Politics: Strategies and Tactics in the Legislative Process* (Rutherford, N.J., 1969), 25–26.

County.[76] Although the east had won a minor victory, it failed to obtain a comprehensive reapportionment on the basis of population.

Some New Jersey residents remained dissatisfied. Writing in 1799 under the pseudonym of "Eumenes," William Griffith published a scathing critique of the state's apportionment system. Griffith claimed, among other things, that the legislature had no right to decide how many representatives each county should receive. Although part of the constitution, this provision left "to *legislative* discretion, [that] which is unquestionably a point of *constitutional* regulation."[77] Griffith objected to the partial reapportionment done in 1797. "This," he said, "may possibly bring the representation to some degree of proportion; but it is evidently imperfect, as in so doing, no common standard of persons, or property can be assumed."[78] Attacking the territorial method of apportionment, he argued, "In short . . . the *majority* do not govern."[79] The solution, he said, lay in adopting a system of representation proportional to population. "The people of New-Jersey," he argued, "will never be secure against partial and unjust deviations from the true principles of representation . . . until [proportional representation] is made an article of the general constitution."[80]

Griffith, however, was one of the few spokesmen for radical change. New Jerseyites were generally content with corporate representation. In fact, since the state's population was relatively evenly dispersed and no vast disparities in area existed among the counties, the method did provide a modicum of equal representation. A modern statistical study has shown that after 1797 inequities in representation among the counties actually declined and remained fairly low well into the nineteenth century.[81] In response to criticism, the legislature made a few slight adjustments in representation in 1804, 1815, and 1818; but it resisted any radical change in the basis of apportionment.[82] Not until 1844, when an entirely new constitution was written, did the state abandon corporate representation altogether.[83] Like citizens in other small states, New Jerseyites had found that territorial apportionment suited their representation needs.

[76]Ibid., 26; William Paterson, comp., *Laws of the State of New Jersey* (New Brunswick, N.J., 1800), 249–50.
[77]Griffith, *Eumenes*, 52.
[78]Ibid.
[79]Ibid., 54.
[80]Ibid.
[81]Ernest C. Reock, Jr., *Population Inequality among Counties in the New Jersey Legislature, 1791–1962* (New Brunswick, N.J., 1963), 14, 19–20.
[82]Ibid., 19.
[83]Thorpe, *Constitutions*, V: 2602.

The Country as Chess Board

Although it is now clear why gross inequities were more likely to develop in large states rather than in smaller ones, it is not so obvious why large states chose to implement numerical apportionment rather than any other method. Certainly the revolutionaries' emphasis on natural rights and individual equality contributed to the development and acceptance of the system. Yet these ideas do not tell the whole story; they do not explain what it was about proportional representation that those in larger states found so appealing.

As they wrote their constitutions, Americans considered and rejected other means of distributing representatives. One proposal simply modified the traditional territorial mode. Retaining the geographic unit as the basis of representation, it required the state to be divided into districts of equal areas. "Abolish their present boundaries," said Joseph Alston of South Carolina, "and let every district in the State comprehend an equal number of square miles, and the evil eventually will not be great."[84] Alston and others hoped that eventually population would be evenly distributed throughout the states, thereby equalizing representation among the units.[85] Supporters of this system justified it by claiming, *"Political bodies should be immortal."*[86] Since population was growing so rapidly, this system would base representation on a stable, unchanging element—the land. The boundaries of the newly drawn districts would remain the same indefinitely. "The method by the number of acres," said a Virginian calling himself "Democraticus," "must be the easiest and most permanent."[87] In many ways, this system appeared to be the logical outgrowth of the traditional, spatial assumptions about representation. Nevertheless, no state chose to reapportion its assembly on this basis.

Americans also considered and dismissed the possibility of basing representation on wealth, as measured by the taxes paid by a district. The low-country members in South Carolina and other southern states gave the most spirited defense of this method. Having fought a Revolu-

[84]Alston, *Speech*, 7.

[85]For examples of the belief that population would eventually be distributed evenly throughout the United States, see Alston, *Speech*, 7; "Anonymous," "The People the Best Governors: Or a Plan of Government Founded on the Just Principles of Natural Freedom" (New Hampshire, 1776), in Hyneman and Lutz, *American Political Writing*, I: 395–96; *The Debates and Proceedings in the Congress of the United States* (Washington, D.C., 1834), I: 801; Loammi Baldwin, *Thoughts on the Study of Political Economy as Connected with the Population, Industry, and Paper Currency of the United States* (New York, 1968; orig. publ. 1809), 15.

[86]"Anonymous," "People the Best Governors," I: 395.

[87]*The (Purdie) Virginia Gazette* (Williamsburg), June 7, 1776.

tion to protect private property, some believed that apportionment in the legislature should reflect this principle. "Representation and taxation should go together," said De Sassure, "and mutually depend on each other."[88] If wealth were the basis of apportionment, communities having more wealth would receive more representatives than other areas.

Yet most Americans had moved beyond the notion that the sole object of representation was to protect private property. They had a broader conception of personal rights and individual liberty. Although two states, Massachusetts and New Hampshire, apportioned their upper houses on the basis of wealth,[89] no state would consider apportioning representation in its lower house—the popular branch— solely on this basis. "I should deplore the degeneracy of spirit, the decay of virtue, the extinction of republicanism, which would be manifested by the adoption of such a system," noted Alston.[90]

How was it, then, that the citizens of the larger states gravitated toward a system of representation based on population? As they set out to devise a method of distributing representation, they considered the characteristics of the population that the new system must accommodate. The population in the large states was rapidly growing, it was widely dispersed, it was spatially mobile, and it was constantly in motion. New areas for settlement were opening up, and the concentration of people was shifting from place to place. Perhaps the greatest difference between the large and small states was the much greater potential for geographic mobility within the boundaries of the large states.

In the revolutionary era, the quickening pace of westward expansion undermined the sense of community that underlay corporate representation. As larger numbers of people moved from place to place, Americans began to question the adequacy of the community as the basic unit of representation. The ideal of a community as a stable, united entity had always been something of a fiction; now Americans saw the notion undermined on a daily basis. Even the very increase of population threatened the communal ideal. "As population increases," noted an American geographer in 1795, "it contracts the spheres of men's actions, and their personal knowledge of Geography will be confined to a few places; to prove this we may only cast our eye to some city or populous town, and there we will find a man transact more business without stepping beyond the limits of a mile, than he who resides in the country by

[88]De Sassure, *Letters on Justice and Expediency*, 6.
[89]Thorpe, *Constitutions*, III: 1895–98; IV: 2459; Adams, *First Constitutions*, 241–42.
[90]Alston, *Speech*, 7.

travelling fifty."[91] People not only were less knowledgeable about their surroundings but less well acquainted with the people who lived nearby. They felt little in common with their neighbors. Physical proximity no longer guaranteed the existence of communal sentiment.

As a result, geographic units, such as counties and towns, came to be seen more as random collections of individuals than as cohesive communities. Alston of South Carolina pointed out: "As population increases . . . or diffuses itself over a greater extent of country, this natural order becomes inconvenient. . . . [These] inconveniences occasion the State, at length, to be divided into districts." These districts, he insisted, are "merely an arrangement for the general *convenience*," not political communities with a life of their own.[92] Communities could not even attempt to speak with a single voice; they contained too many diverse and conflicting interests.

Under such circumstances, the citizens of the larger states saw corporate representation in a new light. The old method appeared static and inflexible, unresponsive to changes in the size and distribution of the population. Just as importantly, people began to see that legislators did not represent geographic units or even whole communities; they represented many diverse interests and individuals. An Englishman had once boasted, "There was scarcely a blade of grass which was not represented" in the House of Commons.[93] But Americans developed other ideas about their legislatures. As a supporter of proportional representation put it, "The *people* of New-Jersey, and not the *counties*, were designed to be represented in the legislature."[94]

To those in states with large territories, numerical apportionment seemed to offer the most appropriate method for representing a rapidly growing, widely dispersed, spatially mobile population. The sense of movement made citizens less attached to particular communities—and to the ideal of community representation. A British reformer once contrasted the American attitude toward proportional representation with the English approach. Englishmen, he claimed, "have always evinced great reluctance to be arbitrarily parcelled out, formed into sections, and divided by metes and bounds, to correspond with a theory, and they

[91]Joseph Scott, *The United States Gazetteer Containing an Authentic Description of the Several States* (Philadelphia, 1795), iii. For a modern discussion of migration patterns, see Theodore J. Crackel, "Longitudinal Migration in America, 1790–1840: A Study of Revolutionary War Pension Records," *Historical Methods*, 14 (1981), 133–37.

[92]Alston, *Speech*, 9.

[93]Pole gives this quote from Lord Chatham and goes on to say, "It seems indeed that the land itself led a political existence independently of the people who lived on it." Pole, *Political Representation*, 444.

[94]Griffith, *Eumenes*, 54.

have commonly cast aside, at the first opportunity, such artificial limits. The advocates of equal electoral divisions . . . will have to surmount great prejudices before they succeed in dividing the country like a chessboard."[95] Americans, especially in larger states, had no such "prejudices" against "dividing the[ir] country like a chess-board." Citizens attending the Essex County Convention of 1776, for example, proclaimed that they had no such "blind Attachment to the Forms of Antiquity"; they were prepared to make radical changes in their methods of distributing representatives.[96]

Moreover, proportional representation could better reflect the greater diversity of interests present in large and growing communities. William Pitt Beers of Connecticut observed in 1791 that, in the past, the lower houses of the legislatures had "represented the people merely in their corporate capacity, not in their diffusive capacity," producing a system that "was calculated rather to check the designs, which were levelled at the liberties of the whole body, than to introduce that detail of wants, feelings and various interests, which, notwithstanding the simplicity of antient manners, take place in every community."[97] In other words, under corporate representation a legislator represented the general interests of the whole community rather than the particular interests of its more specialized parts. Numerical apportionment, which would divide the state into districts based on population, would more likely reflect the various interests found within the state.

Proportional representation changed the whole apportionment process. The state constitution, not the state legislators, prescribed how to divide representation. In time, the system led to the creation of population-based districts, whose boundaries were drawn specifically for representation purposes.[98] Districts were not supposed to constitute organic communities; they were merely arbitrary groupings of individuals. As

[95]Thomas Hare, *The Election of Representatives, Parliamentary and Municipal* (London, 1865), 42–43.

[96]Statement from Essex County Convention (Ipswich), April 25–26, 1776, in Handlin and Handlin, *Popular Sources*, 74.

[97]William Pitt Beers, *An Address to the Legislature and People of the State of Connecticut on the Subject of Dividing the State into Districts for the Election of Representatives in Congress* (New Haven, Conn., 1791), 6.

[98]At first, some states simply granted more representation to existing towns and counties having more people, on the basis of some fixed formula, rather than creating new electoral units. For example, Massachusetts granted each town one representative for every 150 ratable polls, two representatives for every 375 polls, three representatives for every 600 polls, and an additional representative for every additional 225 polls. Thorpe, *Constitutions*, III: 1898. Eventually, however, states abandoned this method in favor of newly created electoral districts based on population. Gordon E. Baker, *State Constitutions: Reapportionment* (New York, 1960), 3–4; Wilder Crane, Jr., and Meredith W. Watts, Jr., *State Legislative Systems* (Englewood Cliffs, N.J., 1968), 24–25.

population levels changed, their boundaries could be redrawn to keep them nearly equal. As people in the large states were realizing, population, not territory, constituted the most important variable in representative institutions.

Apportionment and the States

Throughout the apportionment debates in the states, considerations relating to a state's size impinged on the representation question. The amount of unsettled territory, the variation in population densities throughout the state, the area contained in the political districts, and the population's geographic mobility all contributed to the decision of whether or not to accept proportional representation. Whereas the smaller states faced a situation that was much the same as it had always been, the states having vast western regions confronted an entirely new set of circumstances. They had to find a way to extend representative government to a rapidly growing, widely dispersed, geographically mobile population. As a result, they favored a method of apportionment that could adjust to and accommodate such a population.

Just as significantly, without consulting one another, citizens in states of similar sizes were making the same kinds of decisions about their representative institutions. People in the smaller states continued to think spatially about representation: they placed their state capitals at spots chosen on the basis of geographic factors and retained corporate apportionment for the lower houses of their state legislatures. People in the larger states, in contrast, had begun to define representation issues in demographic terms, locating their capitals at the states' demographic centers and choosing to implement numerical apportionment in their legislatures. A clear split was emerging between the large and the small states. What is more, once delegates from all the states gathered to form a strong national government, they would see for themselves the division's full significance.

CHAPTER 3

The Large State–Small State
Controversy Revisited

The most divisive and troubling issue at the federal Constitutional
Convention was the problem of representation in the national legislature. When delegates from the states met in May 1787 to discuss ways of
strengthening the Union, the Convention split into two factions: the
self-described small states, which favored retaining an equal vote for
each state in Congress, and the self-identified large states, which advocated numerical representation. Although other tensions—between
North and South, East and West, trading and nontrading states existed—the conflict between the large and small states was the one that
almost ended the Convention. "The great difficulty lies in the affair of
Represenation," lamented James Madison three weeks into the proceedings, "and if this could be adjusted, all others would be surmount-
able."[1]

Despite the centrality of this struggle at the Convention and in the
Constitution it produced, historians have tended to dismiss the significance of the large- and small-state coalitions. Some have emphasized the
fundamental agreement on principles among participants at the Convention and the lack of significant ideological differences.[2] Others have
regarded the division as little more than a variation on the sectional

---

[1]Max Farrand, ed., *The Records of the Federal Convention of 1787* (New Haven, Conn.,
1911), I: 321.
[2]John P. Roche, "The Convention as a Case Study in Democratic Politics," in *Essays on
the Making of the Constitution*, ed. Leonard W. Levy (New York, 1969), 175–212; Peter S.
Onuf, *The Origins of the Federal Republic: Jurisdictional Disputes in the United States* (Philadelphia, 1983), 172.

controversy, seeing it as a mask for what they regard as the more important split between North and South.[3] Still others have claimed that the
significance of the division based on size did not extend beyond the
Convention itself.[4]

Yet these interpretations neither examine the conflict in the terms in
which the participants saw it nor place it in the context of the larger,
ongoing struggles over representation at both the state and national
level. Without this examination, the debate seems puzzling, if not unin-
telligible, its terms opaque and its consequences trivial. With this perspective, however, the sources and meaning of the controversy become
strikingly apparent.

The large and the small states clashed over the issue of representation
because each group had come to the federal Convention with a distinctive approach to representation. The delegates from the smaller
states thought spatially about representation questions; those from the
larger states had begun to think about representation in demographic
terms. Once they met at the Convention, they faced a twofold task: to
defend their preconceived ideas about representation and to maximize
their power in the new national legislature. Far from being a product of
simple expediency, the division based on state size reflected the existence of a fundamental cleavage among the states that had resonance
long after the Convention had ended.

Two Alliances

The politics of size first began to emerge at the national level during
the debate over the Articles of Confederation. Certain states proposed
that the states be represented in Congress according to their respective
populations. During sessions in 1776 and 1777, delegates debated the
merits of this proposal. Supporters of the plan voiced arguments similar
to those that would be heard at the federal Convention a decade later.
Attacking the inequities of corporate representation, James Wilson re-

[3]Edmund S. Morgan, *The Birth of the Republic, 1763–89* (Chicago, 1977; orig. publ.
1956), 139–40; Donald L. Robinson, *Slavery in the Structure of American Politics* (New York,
1971), 178–79; Staughton Lynd, *Class Conflict, Slavery and the United States Constitution*
(New York, 1967), 153–83, 185–213; Alfred H. Kelly, Winfred A. Harbison, and Herman
Belz, *The American Constitution: Its Origins and Development*, 6th ed. (New York, 1983), 97–
100.

[4]Kelly and Harbison, *The American Constitution*, 130; Peter S. Onuf, "From Colony to
Territory: Changing Concepts of Statehood in Revolutionary America," *Political Science
Quarterly*, 97 (1982), 459.

marked, "It is strange that annexing the name of 'State' to ten thousand men, should give them an equal right with forty thousand [other men]. This must be the effect of magic, not reason."[5] Supporters also pointed out that only proportional representation could guarantee majority rule. "The interests within doors," asserted John Adams, "should be mathematical representatives of the interests without doors."[6]

Yet numerical, or proportional, representation, as it was called, never succeeded in winning more than limited support, even among the states that would have benefited most from it. On October 7, 1777, when Congress voted on a measure that would have given each state one vote for every fifty thousand white inhabitants, only Pennsylvania and Virginia supported it. A similar scheme establishing a ratio of one representative for every thirty thousand inhabitants also failed.[7] In subsequent years, large-state representatives claimed that the small states had "extorted" the equal-vote provision in the Articles from them.[8] They insisted that the war with England had forced them to capitulate to the desires of the small states. They had "preferred conceding their point . . . ," said one delegate, "to the greater evil of being again reduced to the power of Great Britain."[9] Yet the records themselves indicate that only Virginia consistently backed the proposed system of proportional representation. Although the arguments in favor of this plan were in place as early as 1776, no cohesive group supporting it ever emerged. The large- and small-state coalitions had not yet solidified.

Only after the Articles went to the states for approval did size become an important, and divisive, issue. Legislators from states without western lands began to demand, as a condition for ratification, the creation of a national domain in the West. States with western land claims were to cede these lands to Congress. Profits from their sale would go to support the national legislature. The landless states maintained that men from all the states had fought in and financially supported the Revolution. All Americans, then, should benefit from the western land sales.[10]

---

[5]*Letters of Delegates to Congress, 1774–1789* (Washington, D.C., 1979), IV: 444.

[6]Ibid., IV: 443.

[7]*Journals of Congress* (New York, n.d.), III: 416–17. Rhode Island, Delaware, and Georgia were to receive one vote each until their populations exceeded the requisite number.

[8]Farrand, *Records of the Convention*, I: 552. The phrase is Gouverneur Morris's; his exact statement: "The small States aware of the necessity of preventing anarchy, and taking advantage of the moment, extorted from the large ones an equality of votes."

[9]Edmund C. Burnett, ed., *Letters of Members of the Continental Congress* (Washington, D.C., 1921–1936), VIII: 237.

[10]Onuf, *Origins of the Federal Republic*, 13–15, 151–52; Jack N. Rakove, *The Beginnings of National Politics: An Interpretive History of the Continental Congress* (Baltimore, 1979), 188–91; Merrill Jensen, *The Articles of Confederation* (Madison, Wis., 1966), 192–97.

Small-state representatives believed that a state's size provided an index to its potential population, wealth, and power. In a union composed of states that were vastly unequal in area, the small states claimed to be constantly at risk from their larger neighbors. "The small colonies," said Thomas Stone of Maryland in 1776, "would have no safety if the great Colonies were not limited."[11] Although representatives from the large states denied any intention of hurting the small states, the small-state delegates were not convinced. Only after the larger states had signaled their intention to relinquish their western land claims were the Articles fully ratified.[12] The debate over the Articles had, in effect, confirmed the reality of a division based on state size.

Even after the large states had ceded their western lands, enormous differences in territory remained. To take the most extreme example, Virginia was over one hundred times larger than Rhode Island. Such disparities continued to disturb Americans throughout the Confederation years. Noah Webster pointed out: "The boundaries of the several states were not drawn with a view to independence. . . . The advantages of some states, and the disadvantages of others are so great . . . [that they] materially affect the business and interest of each."[13] In 1786, Thomas Jefferson argued that the new western states should be middling in size, because very large states "would soon crumble into little ones." Americans, he said, "will not only be happier in states of moderate size, but it is the only way in which they can exist as a regular society."[14] As the need for change in the federal government became evident in the 1780s, one writer went so far as to claim that one of the system's main "defects" was in "having some states too large, [and] others more ridiculously small."[15] Political leaders routinely figured state size in the political calculus of the times.

At the Philadelphia Convention, delegates made explicit the distinction between the large and the small states. As antagonistic as the two groups were, the split between them appeared only during discussions of representation questions. Delegates to the Convention, and Americans generally, made a crucial assumption about the relationship be-

[11]John Adams, "Notes of Debates in the Continental Congress," August 2, 1776, in *The Diary and Autobiography of John Adams*, ed. L. H. Butterfield (Cambridge, Mass., 1961), II: 249.

[12]Jensen, *Articles of Confederation*, 192–97; Onuf, *Origins of the Federal Republic*, 75–102.

[13]Noah Webster, *An Examination into the . . . Constitution* (Philadelphia, 1787), 51.

[14]Thomas Jefferson to James Monroe, July 9, 1786, in *The Papers of Thomas Jefferson*, ed. Julian P. Boyd (Princeton, N.J., 1951–), X: 112.

[15]*Cumberland Gazette* (Portland, Mass.), July 19, 1787. See also Onuf, *Origins of the Federal Republic*, 13–15, 34–36, 153.

tween space and population. The delegates believed that the more territory a state possessed, the larger its population could grow. It is important to acknowledge that this position represented an assumption rather than a fact. The rise of modern agriculture, technology, and architecture has invalidated this view, as is evidenced by the appearance of very populous cities that occupy relatively small areas, such as Manhattan, Hong Kong, and Singapore. Yet, in 1787, no one had an inkling of these developments. The delegates were convinced that the smaller states were consigned to a future with fewer people and less wealth than the larger states. At the Convention, then, the small states were trying to avoid having less power as well as less territory.

Delegates to the Convention defined state size in terms of the actual or anticipated population that their territories could support. The large states shared an expectation that their populations were either currently large or had the potential to become large in the near future. The southernmost states—North Carolina, South Carolina, and Georgia—all had extensive unsettled lands and expected to be the great beneficiaries of future population moves.[16] These states joined forces with the three most populous states of the time—Massachusetts, Pennsylvania, and Virginia—to form the large-state coalition.

The small-state alliance, in the words of Luther Martin of Maryland, was composed of those states "whose territory was confined and whose population was at the time large in proportion to their territory."[17] Citizens from these states believed that since they had relatively small areas, their populations would never grow to be much larger than they currently were. As a result, Connecticut, New Jersey, Delaware, and Maryland joined together to form the small-state bloc. New York was the only anomaly. Unlike the other members of the small-state alliance, New York did have western lands into which settlers could move and the potential to support a large population. New York's delegates (with the notable exception of Alexander Hamilton) voted with the small states because they did not wish to alter the Articles in any significant way. Their state had prospered under the Confederation, and they resisted any strengthening of the national government at the state's expense.[18]

[16]Farrand, *Records of the Convention*, I: 605.

[17]Luther Martin, "The Genuine Information, Delivered to the Legislature of the State of Maryland, Relative to the Proceedings of the General Convention, Held at Philadelphia . . . ," in Farrand, *Records of the Convention*, III: 189. Rhode Island did not send delegates to the federal Convention, and New Hampshire's delegates did not arrive until after the vote on the Great Compromise. Because of their small size and area, both states presumably would have joined the small-state alliance had they voted.

[18]Madison's note, in Farrand, *Records of the Convention*, I: 242. See also Clinton Rossiter, *1787: The Grand Convention* (New York, 1967), 93.

The Small States' Maneuver

Historians have traditionally depicted the conflict between large and small states in terms of a power struggle. Under a system of representation based on population, the large states would gain more representatives and would have a significantly greater share of power in Congress. The small states would have their greatest influence only if each state continued to receive an equal vote in the national legislature.[19]

As plausible as this interpretation is, it fails to address a fundamental question. What, specifically, did the small states have to fear from the large states' greater power? If the interests of the large and small states were identical, or even similar, the small states should not have been so threatened by numerical representation. Why, if the distinction between the small and large states was insubstantial, as the large states claimed, were the small states willing to go to the brink of disunion to block the large states' proposal? J. R. Pole suggests that what was at stake was "the force of institutional habit," the small states' greater attachment to the states as political communities.[20] But it is not self-evident why small-state delegates should be more attached to the state community than large-state delegates were.

This is not to suggest that the framers did not care about power. There is no doubt that both the large- and the small-state delegates at the Convention knew about and sought to maximize their power in the Union. But a more complex relationship existed between the delegates' ideas and their interests than has hitherto been suggested.

Soon after the meeting began, the delegates realized that the representation issue presented one of the biggest hurdles they faced in constructing a new national government. Members had to decide whether the new Congress would have one house, as it had under the Articles, or two; who would elect it; and what the basis of apportionment in that legislature should be. Under the original plan, written by James Madison and proposed by Edmund Randolph, representation in both houses would be "proportioned to the Quotas of contribution, or to the number of free inhabitants."[21] As the discussions proceeded, most delegates quickly agreed that there should be a two-chamber legislature that, if numerically proportioned, should be based on population rather than quotas of contribution. Yet other issues remained in dispute.

---

[19]See notes 2, 3, and 4; Rossiter, *1787*, 183, 194; Forrest McDonald, *The Formation of the American Republic, 1776–1790* (Baltimore, Md., 1968), 169–170.

[20]J. R. Pole, *Political Representation in England and the Origins of the American Republic* (New York, 1966), 363, 366.

[21]Farrand, *Records of the Convention*, I: 20.

Because of the different problems, possibilities, and considerations faced by states of vastly different sizes, large- and small-state delegates entered the Convention with very different assumptions about representation. Whereas the small-state representatives approached representation in traditional spatial terms, the large-state delegates espoused the more novel demographic view. As their discussions proceeded, it became clear that neither side wanted to relinquish its view.

The small-state delegates insisted that corporate apportionment was the best and most just form of representation. The community, they believed, was more than the sum of its parts; it was an organic whole. "Each State like each individual," said Roger Sherman of Connecticut, "had its peculiar habits, usages and manners, which constituted its happiness. It would not therefore give to others a power over this happiness, any more than an individual would do, when he could avoid it."[22] The territorial community was the most basic, irreducible unit of representation. As John Lansing of New York reminded those in attendance, "Delegates however chosen, did not represent the people merely as so many individuals; but as forming a sovereign State."[23]

All of the states of the small-state coalition, with the exception of the admittedly anomalous New York, had continued to use corporate representation in their own legislatures.[24] Just as counties or towns were represented in the state assemblies, so states should be represented in the national legislature. Each territorial unit—each state—deserved representation equal to that of every other state in the proposed Congress.

Small-state representatives claimed that corporate representation had at least as much of a claim to legitimacy as the proposed alternative. David Brearly of New Jersey, for example, maintained that "the substitution of a ratio . . . carried fairness on the face of it, but in a deeper examination was unfair and unjust."[25] Historical precedent, the small-state representatives said, supported their position. Because the states had separated from the mother country as states, they subsequently had to relate to one another on that basis. According to Luther Martin: "The separation from G.B. placed the 13 States in a state of nature towards each other; . . . They would have remained in that state till this time, but for the confederation, [which they entered] on the footing of equal-

---

[22]Ibid., I: 343.
[23]Ibid., I: 336.
[24]Francis N. Thorpe, comp., *The Federal and State Constitutions, Colonial Charters, and Other Organic Laws of the States, Territories, and Colonies Now or Heretofore Forming the United States of America* (Washington, D.C., 1909), I: 536–46, 563; IV: 1691, 1693–94; V: 2595.
[25]Farrand, *Records of the Convention*, I: 177.

ity."[26] William Paterson of New Jersey warned of the dangers of altering that original compact. "When independent societies confederate for mutual defense," he said, "they do so in their collective capacity; and then each state for those purposes must be considered as *one* of the contracting parties. Destroy this balance of equity, and you endanger the rights of *lesser* societies by the danger of usurpation in the greater."[27] The original equality among the states, the small-state delegates argued, should be the basis for any continuing union among them.

Early in the Convention, the small-state delegates made a surprising proposal. They agreed to accept proportional representation in both houses of the national legislature if—and only if—Congress would eliminate current state boundaries. The states would be reconstituted, with each containing approximately the same amount of land. "Lay the map of the confederation on the table," said David Brearly on June 9, "and extinguish the present boundary lines of the respective state jurisdictions, and make a new division so that each state is equal."[28]

This plan can best be explained in terms of the small states' spatial assumptions about representation. Under the large states' plan for proportional representation, vast disparities in state size would translate into vast differences in representation. States with more area and more potential for population growth would receive many more representatives than states whose territory was limited and whose population would never be very large. The small states' audacious redivision of territory would help mitigate this injustice. "If we are to be considered as a nation," argued William Paterson, "all State distinctions must be abolished, the whole must be thrown into a hotchpot, and when an equal division is made, then there may be fairly an equality of representation."[29] Equalization of territory, according to small-state delegates, would result in more nearly equal populations among the states—and hence more equal representation. Even John Dickinson of Delaware agreed: "Throw all Governments and Territories into Common Stock and divide de novo. Then we shall have the Equity and Equality talked of[,] not otherwise."[30] If the small states were to face a threat to their corporate existence, they would meet it on their own terms.

The large-state delegates quickly observed the plan's revolutionary nature and rejected it out-of-hand. Most labeled it "impracticable" and

[26]Ibid., I: 324.
[27]Ibid., I: 259.
[28]Ibid., I: 182.
[29]Ibid., I: 178.
[30]John Dickinson, "Notes for a Speech, June 30 (?), 1787," in "John Dickinson at the Federal Constitutional Convention," ed. James H. Hutson, *William & Mary Quarterly*, 3d. ser., 40 (1983), 277.

not worthy of detailed consideration.[31] "The dissimilarities existing in the rules of property, as well as in the manners, habits, and prejudices of the different States, amounted to a prohibition of the attempt," insisted James Madison of Virginia, sounding very much like a small-state member.[32] In one of the few substantive responses, Benjamin Franklin pointed out that an equal division of territory would not necessarily produce equality of representation among the states. If the number of inhabitants in the states changed, another division would be necessary to keep the representation equal.[33] Furthermore, the large states, like the small, would no longer exist in their present form—a possibility their delegates were not willing to accept. Finally, large-state members realized that under such a system, numerical representation would give them no substantial advantage over the other states.

It is impossible to say with certainty whether or not the small states were bluffing. The small-state delegates probably suspected that the large states would oppose the scheme and offered it as a tactical maneuver to expose the element of self-interest behind the large states' support for proportional representation. Furthermore, they hoped to demonstrate that even large-state delegates had some respect for the states as territorial communities.

Whether or not the small-state delegates were bluffing, the plan vividly demonstrated the logic of corporate representation. As they saw it, territorial units formed the irreducible basis of representation. Even if the states no longer existed in their present form, the state would still remain the unit of representation. Equalizing the states' areas would help equalize population and, ultimately, representation. A similar proposal had been made in some of the states. A Virginia writer who called himself "Democraticus" had suggested in 1776, for example, that redrawing county boundary lines to give each unit the same total area would solve the state's apportionment problem.[34] Although no state had adopted the plan, the small-state representatives may have seen it as a genuine alternative to a proposal that threatened both their power and their existence. In the end, however, the small states' startling proposal went nowhere.

In contrast to the small-state delegates, the large-state delegates thought about representation in demographic terms. Population rather than territory formed the basis of representation; the individual rather than the community constituted the basic unit of representation. "The

[31]Farrand, *Records of the Convention*, I: 321–23.
[32]Ibid., I: 321.
[33]Ibid., I: 199.
[34]*The (Purdie) Virginia Gazette* (Williamsburg), June 7, 1776.

Genl. Govt.," asserted James Wilson of Pennsylvania, "is not an assemblage of States, but of individuals for certain political purposes—it is not meant for the States, but for the individuals composing them; the *individuals* therefore [and] not the *States*, ought to be represented in it."[35]

Many of the large-state delegates had firsthand experience with numerical representation in their own states. Among the six states composing the large-state coalition, three—Massachusetts, Pennsylvania, and South Carolina—had accepted the principle of numerical apportionment by the time of the federal Convention.[36] In contrast, only one of the five small states—the anomalous New York—had adopted the method. "There was the same reason for different numbers of representatives from different States," insisted Madison, "as from Counties of different extents within the particular States."[37] What Madison and the other large-state members ignored, however, was the fact that most of the small states had not accepted proportional representation in their legislatures—and were not now prepared to accept it for the national legislature.

Large-state delegates firmly believed that proportional representation was the most just, fair, and republican method of apportioning representatives. They noted that the corporate system might result in a majority of states contravening the wishes of a majority of the people. "The injustice of allowing each State an equal vote," contended Elbridge Gerry of Massachusetts, "was long [ago] insisted on."[38] The large-state delegates emphasized the importance of majority rule. The states "ought to vote," said James Madison, "in the same proportion as their citizens would do, if the people of all the States were collectively met."[39] Proportional representation would correct the inequities caused by corporate apportionment. According to James Wilson of Pennsylvania, justice demanded that "equal numbers of people ought to have an equal number of representatives, and different numbers of people different numbers of representatives."[40]

Although large-state members claimed to see no diversity of interests between the two groups, small-state representatives remained acutely sensitive on this point. Delegate John Lansing of New York pointed out,

[35]Farrand, *Records of the Convention*, I: 406.

[36]See chapter 2. Because of opposition from its eastern elite, South Carolina accepted the principle of numerical representation in its 1778 constitution but did not actually implement the system until 1808.

[37]Farrand, *Records of the Convention*, I: 37. See also I: 180.

[38]Ibid., I: 467.

[39]Ibid., I: 562.

[40]Ibid., I: 179.

"If it were true that a uniformity of interests existed among the States, there was equal safety for them all, whether representation remained as heretofore, or were proportioned as now proposed."[41] Maryland's Luther Martin echoed Lansing's position: "If the large States have the same interest with the smaller as was urged, there could be no danger in giving them an equal vote."[42] If both sides' interests were truly compatible, then numerical apportionment should not have been such a bone of contention. The fact that it was suggests that a real diversity—or perception of diversity—of interests existed. What exactly, then, were the small states afraid of?

According to the small-state representatives, concrete, specific interests differentiated the large states from the small. Communities of similar size, they said, had similar interests and those of different sizes, differing interests. Under a system of numerical apportionment, the larger states would have the power to impose their will on the smaller. In regard to trade and commerce, for example, the large states could promote their own states' fortunes at the small states' expense. "Suppose that in pursuance of some commercial treaty or arrangement," declared Oliver Ellsworth of Connecticut, "three or four free ports & no more were to be established[.] [W]ould not combinations be formed in favor of Boston—Phila. && some port in Chesapeak?" Although, when pressed, Ellsworth admitted that "no particular abuses could be foreseen," he still believed that "the possibility of them would be sufficient to alarm" him.[43]

The July 10 proposal of Virginian Edmund Randolph, called "Suggestions for Conciliating the Small States," was more explicit about such concerns. Under Randolph's scheme, Congress would still be apportioned according to population, but in certain instances each state would receive an equal vote. These instances would include the disposition of the western territories, the admission of new states into the Union, the location of the new national capital, and the extension of citizenship rights to new states.[44] Although Randolph's plan was never reported out of committee, it revealed that both large- and small-state delegates had at least some awareness of the issues that most alarmed the small states.

The small states' resistance to proportional representation went far beyond the question of narrow economic and political self-interest, and it could not be overcome by a compromise that did not directly deal with

[41] Ibid., I: 337.
[42] Ibid., I: 445.
[43] Ibid., I: 484–85.
[44] "Edmund Randolph's Suggestions for Conciliating the Small States," July 10, 1787, in Farrand, *Records of the Convention*, III: 55–56.

the central issue: the states' differing approaches to representation. The tone of the small states' arguments verged on hysteria. The larger states, the small states said, would form "a solid column indeed, a formidable phalanx" that would "crush the small ones whenever they stand in the way of their ambitions or interested views."[45] In promoting numerical apportionment, the large states were acting from "interested and . . . ambitious motives," intending to exercise absolute control over the small states and seeking to "swallow all of them up," or make them "enslaved" to their larger neighbors.[46] Proportional representation was not only not safe for the smaller states, it was downright "dangerous."[47]

At the most basic level, numerical representation posed a threat to the small states' territorial integrity. If the large states had overwhelming control of Congress, there was nothing they could not do—including eliminate the small states. Small-state delegates had no reason to believe that the large states would not take full advantage of their superiority and therefore imagined the worst. William Paterson of New Jersey "considered the proposition for a proportional representation as striking at the existence of the lesser states."[48] An equal vote in at least one branch of the legislature was necessary, according to Roger Sherman of Connecticut, "otherwise three or four of the large States would rule the others as they please."[49] "The power of defense was essential to the small states," emphasized Oliver Ellsworth of Connecticut. "Nature," he continued, "had given it to the smallest insect of the creation. [I could] never admit that there was no danger of combinations among the large States. They will like individuals find out and avail themselves of the advantage gained by it."[50] William Samuel Johnson of Connecticut expressed the small states' bottom line. "The fact is," he said, "that the States do exist as political Societies, and a Govt. is to be formed for them in their political capacity, as well as for the individuals composing them. Does it not seem to follow that if the States as such are to exist they must be armed with some power of self-defence[?]"[51]

According to small-state representatives, the adoption of numerical representation in both houses of the legislature would leave their states

[45]The two speakers, in order, were Brearly on June 9 and Bedford on June 8. Farrand, *Records of the Convention*, I: 167, 177.

[46]The speakers, in order, were Bedford on June 30, Read on June 6, and Madison on June 28. Farrand, *Records of the Convention*, I: 500, 136, 445. For similar language, see ibid., I: 177, 341.

[47]Farrand, *Records of the Convention*, I: 444–45.

[48]Ibid., I: 177.

[49]Ibid., I: 343.

[50]Ibid., I: 469.

[51]Ibid., I: 461.

defenseless and ultimately would lead to their demise. It could be argued that these fears were groundless, but there is no denying the sense of panic that led the representatives to cling, ever more desperately, to their position. The small states needed—and thought they deserved—some means of protecting their statehood against potential assaults by the large states.

For at least the first month of the Convention, the large- and small-state delegates talked past each other. Because their assumptions about representation differed so fundamentally, they could find no common ground of cooperation or agreement. Only a shift to radically different tactics could break the deadlock.

Arbitrary Lines and Imaginary Beings

Because they were working from a position of relative weakness, the small states had to concede a great deal early in the Convention. On June 11, the small states had suffered a crushing blow. A majority of the states had approved a resolution establishing numerical representation for both the upper and lower houses of the national legislature.[52] The small-state delegates faced a crucial decision. Because they could not tolerate this system in both houses, they had to either leave the Convention in protest or remain for a time, hoping to persuade the large-state delegates to allow an equal vote in at least one house. The small-state members chose to stay. But they had reached a point from which they would not retreat. They had, in effect, made their biggest concession of the Convention.

Shortly afterwards, William Paterson of New Jersey made one last attempt for the small states. Under his proposal, Congress would remain a unicameral body and each state would continue to receive one vote.[53] Voicing the small states' displeasure with the proceedings, he warned that members of his faction "would rather submit to a monarch, to a despot, than to such a fate" as they would face under the Randolph plan.[54] But at least some small-state delegates knew that they would eventually have to compromise. John Dickinson of Delaware predicted that the dispute among the states "must probably end in mutual concession. He hoped that each State would retain an equal voice in at least one branch of the National Legislature."[55] With the defeat of Paterson's

[52]Ibid., I: 195.
[53]Ibid., I: 242–45.
[54]Ibid., I: 179.
[55]Ibid., I: 87.

program, the small states' best hope lay in the possible acceptance of corporate representation in one house of the legislature.

At first, however, no one was in a compromising mood. Each side viewed the other's position with incomprehension. Like many other large-state delegates, Edmund Randolph believed that "the danger apprehended by the little states was chimerical."[56] These delegates believed that the small states were being irrationally obstinate. If, however, the large states were baffled by the small states' attachment to spatial representation, then the small states were equally baffled by the large states' demographic approach to representation questions. Luther Martin of Maryland expressed the small states' sense of disbelief. "The language of the States being *sovereign* and *independent*, was once familiar & understood," he said, "though it seemed now so strange & obscure."[57] Because the small-state delegates had not accepted the principle of numerical representation in their own states, they believed the large states were using the method simply to dupe them.

As the proceedings dragged on, the large-state delegates concluded that they must alter their methods and challenge the small states' anachronistic assumptions about representation. These outdated premises, they thought, prevented the small states from seeing the greater advantages of proportional apportionment. If they could decisively discredit the whole spatial approach, the small states would quickly accede to their proposals.

The distinction based on state size framed—but impeded—the debate. As part of their attack, the large-state members argued that size did not, in fact, represent an important division among states. History, they said, proved that large states competed with one another more often than they cooperated. Carthage and Rome, Austria and France, England and France—all provided examples of states that vied with each other for prominence instead of subduing their smaller neighbors.[58] Closer to home, size alone had never produced alliances, either within states or among them. "It had never been seen," said Madison, "that different Counties in the same State, conformable in extent, but disagreeing in other circumstances, betrayed a propensity to such combinations."[59] Even during the Confederation years, states of the same size had not voted together in Congress.

The large-state delegates also attempted to show the unlikelihood of a conspiracy of large states against small. Important economic differences

[56]Ibid., II: 55.
[57]Ibid., I: 468.
[58]Ibid., I: 447–50.
[59]Ibid., I: 448.

divided the large states. Hundreds of miles and diverse economic interests came between the three largest states—Massachusetts, Pennsylvania, and Virginia. These states, commented Alexander Hamilton, "were separated from each other by distance of place, and equally so, by all the peculiarities which distinguish the interest of one State from those of another."[60] Massachusetts produced fish, Pennsylvania marketed wheat, and Virginia sold tobacco as its primary crop.[61] An alliance among these states was unfeasible as well as unlikely. Even if some combination were to occur, the large-state delegates said, the remaining states would have the power within Congress to defeat it.[62]

Continuing their assault, the large states insisted that there was no great difference of interests among states of different sizes. No state was a distinctive community, existing as an independent economic or cultural unit. Interests and values crossed state lines, uniting all Americans. "We are now one nation of brethren," said James Wilson of Pennsylvania. "We must bury all local interests & distinctions."[63] The boundaries between states were merely arbitrary lines on a map, the worn artifacts of British rule. The colonies, said Gouverneur Morris of Pennsylvania, "were originally nothing more than colonial corporations."[64] Since the Revolution, boundaries possessed far less meaning than they had previously had. "Formerly, indeed," observed Benjamin Franklin, "when almost every province had a different Constitution, some with greater, others with fewer privileges, it was of importance to the borderers when their boundaries were contested, whether by running division lines, they were placed on one side or the other. At present when such differences are done away, it is less material."[65] By emphasizing the distinctiveness of each state, small-state representatives failed to see the larger community of interests uniting all Americans.

Because the states did not constitute discrete communities, they did not deserve representation on this basis. According to the large-state members, the states were "artificial beings" and state sovereignty was a "phantom" or "wonderful illusion."[66] "States," said Alexander Hamil-

---

[60]Ibid., I: 325.
[61]Ibid., I: 447–48.
[62]Ibid., I: 325.
[63]Ibid., I: 166.
[64]Ibid., I: 552.
[65]Ibid., I: 199. William Byrd's classic *History of the Dividing Line between Virginia and North Carolina as Run in 1728–29* (Richmond, Va., 1866) provides support for Franklin's claim about the greater significance of colonial boundaries. Byrd noted: "Wherever we passed we constantly found Borderers laid it to Heart if their Land was taken into Virginia: They chose much rather to belong to Carolina where they pay no Tribute, either to God or to Caesar." I: 65.
[66]Farrand, *Records of the Convention*, I: 466, 489–90.

ton, "are a collection of individual men[.] [W]hich ought we to respect most, the rights of the people composing them, or of the artificial beings resulting from the composition[?]"[67] The people, rather than fictive entities, should be represented. "Can we forget," asked James Wilson, "for whom we are forming a Government? Is it for *men,* or for the imaginary beings called *States?*"[68] Population, the large-state delegates urged, should be the basis of representation in a republic.

The small states were unimpressed. In reply to the assertion that the large states would never hurt the small, Gunning Bedford of Delaware retorted, "I do not, gentlemen, trust you." To the claim that the large states tended to compete rather than cooperate with one another, Bedford responded, "This, I repeat, is language calculated only to amuse us."[69] Nothing the large-state delegates could say could convince the small states that the spatial approach to representation was outmoded. The small states had already made a major concession by staying at the Convention and listening to such talk. They would simply wait for the large states to make some tangible offer.

Madison's Miscalculation

After almost a month of fruitless discussion, the large-state delegates were becoming desperate. Because they wanted to jolt the small states out of their spatial assumptions about representation, they hoped to shatter the distinction based on state size. On June 29, Hamilton pointed to the existence of a division more important than the cleavage between the large and small states. "The only considerable distinction of interests," he said, lay between "the carrying & non-carrying States"—that is, between the states that engaged in trade and those that did not.[70]

Madison picked up on Hamilton's point the next day but took it in a new direction. He too believed there was a division more important than that between the large states and the small—not between the carrying and noncarrying states, as Hamilton had suggested, but between the slave and the free states. "The states," Madison said, "were divided into different interests not by their differences of size but by other circumstances; the most material of which resulted partly from climate, but principally from the effects of their having or not having slaves. These two causes concurred in the great division of interests in the U.

[67]Ibid., I: 466.
[68]Ibid., I: 483.
[69]Ibid., I: 500.
[70]Ibid., I: 466.

States. It did not lie between the large & small States: It lay between the Northern & Southern."[71] Because he made size interests seem irrelevant, Madison could offer a method of apportioning representatives that he believed would help balance northern and southern interests in the national legislature.[72]

In his speech, Madison used sectionalism as a means of extricating the Convention from its current impasse. As potentially divisive as the slavery issue was, Madison did not believe he risked too much by drawing attention to it. Slavery in 1787 was not, as historian Max Farrand observed, "the moral question that it later became."[73] Sectional allegiance did not have any discernible effect on the apportionment debates. Throughout the first half of the Convention, none of the votes on representation questions—not even the vote on the question of counting slaves as three-fifths of whites—divided along sectional lines.[74] (See appendix 2.) Madison knew that for delegates at the Convention, state size was a more real and more volatile issue than slavery.

Historians praise Madison for his foresight, declaring that he was one of the few delegates "who saw the really fundamental conflict in American society at the time."[75] Yet Madison's speech was less an act of great insight than a last-ditch attempt to salvage the Convention. Although Madison believed that sectionalism was "but too apt to arise of itself,"[76] he turned the representatives' attention to it only in the hope that the small states would see that their long-term interests did not depend on

[71]Ibid., I: 486.

[72]Ibid., I: 486–87.

[73]Max Farrand, *The Framing of the Constitution of the United States* (New Haven, Conn., 1970; orig. publ. 1913), 110.

[74]In fact, the only vote taken during the first half of the Convention that was decided along sectional lines was on a simple procedural matter—whether or not to postpone discussion of the government's power until after the representation issue had been settled. See Donald L. Robinson, "Slavery and Sectionalism in the Founding of the United States, 1787–1808" (diss., Cornell University, 1966), 109. I obviously disagree with Staughton Lynd's contention that the "sectional conflict between North and South was the major tension at the Convention," in *Class Conflict, Slavery and the U.S. Constitution,* 160. It is worth remembering that the three-fifths figure for counting blacks was arrived at in 1783, when the Confederation Congress sought a new method of apportioning taxes. See "Amendment to Share Expenses According to Population," 18 April 1783, in *The Documentary History of the Ratification of the Constitution,* ed. Merrill Jensen (Madison, Wis., 1976), I: 148–50. Although the slavery issue was important and divisive, particularly during the second half of the Convention, it did not nearly cause the meeting to break up, as the apportionment question did.

[75]Robert E. Brown, "The Beard Thesis Attacked: A Political Approach," in Levy, *Essays on the Making of the Constitution,* 103. In *Framing of the Constitution,* Farrand said on p. 110, "Madison was one of the very few men who seemed to appreciate the real divisions of interest in this country." See also Onuf, *Origins of the Federal Republic,* 171–72, for a more balanced view.

[76]Farrand, *Records of the Convention,* I: 487.

size. He was certain that once he had revealed the real and inevitable "line of discrimination"[77] among the states, they would come to their senses and abandon their insistence on territorial apportionment. State size, he implied, was merely a transitory division among the states.

Whatever Madison's long-term perspicacity, his short-term strategy backfired. His speech swayed the wrong people. In the weeks after June 30, the small-state delegates continued to vote with their chosen coalition and made no comment on the North-South division. But the large-state delegates did remark on the issue's significance—and appeared to see the Convention proceedings in a new way. On July 10, for example, Rufus King of Massachusetts reported that he "was fully convinced that the question concerning a difference of interests did not lie where it had hitherto been discussed, between the great & small States; but between the Southern & Eastern. For this reason he had been ready to yield something in the proportion of representation for the security of the Southern [interests]."[78] On July 13, Gouverneur Morris of Pennsylvania remarked, "A distinction had been set up & urged, between the Nn. & Southn. States." Whereas he had "hitherto considered the doctrine as heretical," he saw that southerners "persisted" in making it. Thus it must have validity.[79] Only two days before the vote on the Great Compromise, Madison commented, "It seemed now to be pretty well understood that the real difference of interests lay, not between the large & small but between the N. & Southn. States."[80] Yet, according to comments that Madison himself recorded, the only members who appeared to be convinced were those from large states. Madison, it seems, had weakened his own alliance and aided the opposition he had hoped to undermine.

Not coincidentally, the large-state coalition began to splinter and dissolve shortly after Madison's speech. Two days after the speech, the Convention voted on a resolution to establish an equal vote in the second branch of the legislature. Although the large states had defeated the measure on June 11, it was reconsidered on July 2. This time the large states could manage only a tie vote.[81] Georgia, previously a faithful member of the large-state contingent, split its vote, creating the deadlock. (See appendix 2.) At this point, Roger Sherman of Connecticut declared that the proceedings had come to a "full stop."[82] A special committee was formed to find a solution to the crisis.

The dissolution of the large-state coalition continued. On July 7,

---

[77]Ibid., II: 10.
[78]Ibid., I: 566.
[79]Ibid., I: 604. See also I: 601.
[80]Ibid., II: 9–10.
[81]Ibid., I: 192–95, 509–10.
[82]Ibid., I: 511.

members voted on whether the equal-vote provision should be included in the special committee's report. Once again, the large-state delegation split, with North Carolina switching to the small-state position. The Massachusetts and Georgia contingents could not agree among themselves and thus could not cast a vote for either side.[83] On July 14 delegates voted on the terms of admission for new states. The proposal stipulated that the number of representatives from new states could never exceed the number from the original states. A second, inferior class of states would be created, protecting the existing states.[84] This vote threw the large-state coalition into complete disarray. Massachusetts supported the measure, and the Pennsylvania delegation split its vote. The plan failed, but the large states were no longer voting together on representation issues. Throughout all these votes, however, the small-state coalition had remained intact.[85] (See appendix 2.)

By July 16, it was all over. Key defections from the large-state coalition enabled the Great Compromise to pass. Members voted not just on the apportionment of Congress but also on a whole package. The package included provisions making representation proportional to taxes and taxes proportional to population, requiring a decennial census, giving the lower house the exclusive right to originate money bills, and counting slaves as three-fifths of whites for the purpose of representation.[86] Despite the inclusion of other provisions, this fact seemed to have had little effect on the outcome. Each state voted as it had on the equal-vote resolution of July 7—with the exception of Georgia, which rejoined the large-state ranks. The four small states—Connecticut, New Jersey, Delaware, and Maryland—joined by the large state North Carolina voted for the package; Pennsylvania, Virginia, South Carolina, and Georgia voted against it. Massachusetts divided its vote. (Delegates from the "small" state of New York had left the Convention before the vote was taken.) The defection of North Carolina and Massachusetts from the large-state ranks had provided the bare margin necessary for the Compromise to pass. (See appendix 2.)

The timing of the large-state collapse indicates that Madison's June 30 speech played a crucial role in its demise. Inadvertently, Madison had convinced his own allies that their coalition was not as important as

[83]Ibid., II: 1–2.

[84]Ibid. The exact wording of the proposal was: "That to secure the liberties of the States already confederated, the number of representatives in the first branch, shall never exceed the representatives from such of the thirteen united states as shall accede to this Confederacy."

[85]The only defection from the small-state camp was New Jersey, which voted against the proposal regarding admission of new states. All the other small states voted for the motion and voted together on other representation questions. (See appendix 2.)

[86]Farrand, *Records of the Convention*, II: 13–15.

they had thought. Delegates from the large states knew that the small states had already made a major concession in accepting proportional representation for the lower house, whereas they themselves had relinquished nothing. They also understood that the Convention's most important goal was to strengthen the Union and that they should not get sidetracked by subordinate issues. Madison's speech suggested to them that their alliance with the other large states was merely transitory in nature. The North-South split appeared to be the more enduring division. Why, then, should they risk the Convention's dissolution just to win their point in both houses of Congress? With the help of Madison's formulation, the large-state delegates saw that their alliance and what it stood for was not worth the risk to the Union's future.

After the Compromise had passed, the large states reached the same point that the small states had come to on June 11: concede or leave, give in or give up. Because the large states possessed the bulk of the country's people and territory, they had resisted the idea of compromise. They had been certain they could force the small states to capitulate.[87] But the small states would not budge any further than they already had. "The little States were fixed," said John Rutledge of South Carolina after the vote on the Compromise. "They had repeatedly & solemnly declared themselves to be so. All that the large States then had to do, was to decide whether they would yield or not."[88]

It was now up to the large states. On the morning after the vote, certain large-state delegates met privately to discuss their alternatives. Despite their unhappiness, they could reach no conclusion—other than to swallow the bitter pill they had been offered. "The time was wasted in vague conversation on the subject," noted James Madison, "without any specific proposition or agreement."[89] By returning to the Convention, the representatives signaled their acceptance of the Compromise. As the small states had done earlier, the large states decided that they could live with their opponents' conception of representation.

The Controversy Institutionalized

The intensity of the large state–small state controversy surprised the Convention participants. Although the two groups had previously made

---

[87]For example, on June 9, James Wilson had declared, "If the small states will not confederate on this [the Randolph] plan, Pena. & . . . some other States, would not confederate on any other." Farrand, *Records of the Convention*, I: 180.

[88]Ibid., II: 19.

[89]Ibid., II: 19–20.

separate choices in representative institutions in their own states, they had not realized how these decisions would affect their approach to national government. Only when they gathered in a national forum did it become clear that a formal distinction between the groups was the basis for a far-reaching dispute.

State size had produced a difference in principles and in perspective between the large and small states. Circumstances that had made corporate representation eminently reasonable in the small states also made it seem logical for the national legislature. Conditions in the larger states, however, had forced the large-state members to begin to think demographically about representation issues. Because they used population as the basis for their state institutions, they thought it reasonable that the nation use the method as well. Beyond that, each side also knew that its particular approach was uniquely suited to maximizing its power and advancing its principles. Yet, because more than simple expediency was involved, each side was willing to go to the brink of disunion for its cause.

By September 1787, the Convention had succeeded in producing a new Constitution. Both coalitions had agreed to a compromise that recognized proportional representation in one house and corporate representation in the other. Although neither side was perfectly happy, it was a solution both could tolerate.

Ironically, however, the compromise itself had effectively institutionalized the division based on state size. With the large states having a majority in the lower house and the small states having disproportionate influence in the upper, the struggle between the two factions could continue indefinitely. And as subsequent events showed, under certain circumstances it would.

CHAPTER 4

Representation and
the Extensive Republic

The debates over capital removal, apportionment in the state legislatures, and representation in Congress all expressed different aspects of
the division between the large and small states. As legislators made their
decisions, they took into account the area and population of the state
they represented, weighing all that that implied in terms of the state's
problems, future possibilities, and power relative to other states. The
decisions they reached reflected the fact that states having very large
areas and populations needed different kinds of representative institutions than did states that were much smaller. In time, the differences
that had developed between the large and small states erupted into
conflict at the federal Constitutional Convention—a conflict that, although temporarily resolved, would resurface in coming years.

Paradoxically, however, the division between the large and small
states did not carry over to the debate over the Constitution, for several
reasons. First, as John Roche has demonstrated, the small states were as
committed as the large to strengthening the federal government at the
Philadelphia Convention.[1] They had demanded—and ultimately received—an equal vote in one house of the new national legislature.
Once they won their point, they had no fundamental objections to the
proposed government and did not seek to block the Constitution's
ratification. The small states approved the Constitution as quickly as, if

---

[1]John P. Roche, "The Convention as a Case Study in Democratic Politics," in *Essays on
the Making of the Constitution*, ed. Leonard W. Levy (New York, 1969), 186–200.

not more quickly than, the larger states.[2] If large-state Antifederalists sometimes appropriated small-state arguments in opposing the Constitution, they made those arguments for very different reasons than did small-state representatives at the Convention. Whereas small-state delegates had always been committed to fortifying the Union, large-state Antifederalists often were not.

Even more importantly, the division based on state size emerged only under specific conditions—that is, in the context of debates over institutions of representative government. The conflict was never popularly based; it was always confined to representative bodies. Even there, it surfaced only when delegates discussed matters relating to the election or distribution of representatives. Yet representation composed only a small part of the debate over the Constitution. As wide-ranging and extensive as it was, the ratification debate did not generate the particular circumstances in which the division based on size would become operative.

It would be a mistake, though, to see no connection between the two controversies. In the large state–small state conflicts, size had been a determinative factor in shaping representative institutions. In the debate between the Federalists and Antifederalists over an extended republic, size *was* the issue.

The Antifederalists opposed the expansion of a single republican government to all thirteen states—and predicted disaster if it were attempted. More sanguine, the Federalists believed that the effort, although "unprecedented,"[3] was "the fairest experiment that had been ever made in favor of human nature."[4] In *Federalist* No. 14, James Madison made an emotional plea for the document. "Is the experiment of an extended republic to be rejected merely because it may comprise what is new?" he asked. "Is not the glory of the people of America that, whilst they have paid a decent regard to the opinions of former times and other nations, they have not suffered a blind veneration for antiquity, for custom, or for names, to overrule the suggestions of their own good sense, the knowledge of their own situation, and the lessons of their own experience?"[5] The more cautious Antifederalists, however, warned: "A

[2]The order of ratification was Delaware, Pennsylvania, New Jersey, Georgia, Connecticut, Massachusetts, Maryland, South Carolina, New Hampshire, Virginia, New York, North Carolina, and Rhode Island. See Forrest McDonald, *The Formation of the American Republic, 1776–1790* (Baltimore, Md., 1965), 209–36.

[3]Jonathan Elliot, ed., *The Debates in the Several State Conventions, on the Adoption of the Federal Constitution* . . . (Washington, D.C., 1937), III: 94.

[4]Ibid., IV: 262.

[5]Alexander Hamilton, John Jay, and James Madison, *The Federalist*, ed. Jacob E. Cooke (Middletown, Conn., 1961; orig. publ. 1788), 88.

wise nation will . . . attempt innovations of this kind with much circum-
spection. They will view the political fabric, which they have once
reared, as the sacred *palladium* of their happiness."[6] If the experiment
failed, "Alfred" advised, "our liberties might fail with it."[7] Although
other parts of the Constitution might be amended, deleted, or rewritten,
the document presumed the existence of an extended republic. When
the Antifederalists attacked this premise, they were attacking the new
government's very foundation. Both sides knew that winning this argument might determine their success in the wider struggle over the
Constitution.

In a very different way from the previous controversies, representation lay at the heart of the conflict over an extensive republic. Whereas
other representation disputes focused on the structure of representative
institutions, this one was more theoretical; it discussed in more general
terms the proper relationship between space and representation. Whereas the Antifederalists believed effective representation could exist only
in a small area, the supporters of the Constitution redefined the representatives' and constituents' roles in such a way as to make space irrelevant to representation. The Federalists showed that, at the most fundamental level, representation in a republic was relative to population
rather than territory.

The account rendered here imposes a logic on Federalist and Antifederalist thought that, although implicit throughout what each side
wrote, was not necessarily expressed in every article or pamphlet. These
ideas did not constitute systematic ideologies; they were instead an
evolving set of working hypotheses. Moreover, many issues besides
representation divided the Federalists from the Antifederalists—for example, their attitudes toward individual liberty, states' rights, and the
role of a natural aristocracy in governing. Yet the differences over representation were basic to their larger disagreements—and the resolution of
these differences marked an important watershed in the development of
American ideas about representative government.

The Reach of Every Citizen

The Antifederalist criticisms of an extensive republic and the Constitution that would create it grew out of the Antifederalists' spatial

---

[6]"Essays by The Impartial Examiner," *Virginia Independent Chronicle*, February 20, 1788,
in *The Complete Anti-Federalist*, ed. Herbert J. Storing, with the editorial assistance of
Murray Dry (Chicago, 1981), V: 174 (hereafter cited as *CA*).
[7]"Alfred," in *CA*, III: 143.

assumptions about government. In many ways, theirs were the conventional assumptions of the age in which they lived. In support of their view, the Antifederalists cited history, political theory, and their own experience.

As good students of the Enlightenment, the Antifederalists believed that history had lessons that could be applied to modern-day politics.[8] According to the Antifederalists, a study of the past indicated that republican government was incompatible with extensive territory. The ancient Greek city-states, as well as the Roman republic, had encompassed relatively small areas. Over time, however, these nations had expanded their boundaries and, in the process, lost their republican governments. According to "Brutus," they "extended their conquests over large territories of country: and the consequence was, that their governments were changed from that of free governments to those of the most tyrannical that ever existed in the world."[9] If the United States wished to preserve its own republican tradition, it should heed the lessons of the past.

The Antifederalists also cited political philosophers, ranging from Aristotle to Shaftesbury, who confirmed their view that republics must be limited in area.[10] They particularly admired and quoted Montesquieu, who spoke directly to the relationship between a state's size and its proper form of government. In *The Spirit of Laws*, he argued that small areas were most appropriate for republics and middling-sized areas were suitable for monarchies. Extremely large areas could support either a despotism or a confederacy composed of several smaller states.[11] Montesquieu warned, however, that if a republic extended itself beyond natural limits, it would fall into the hands of a dictator or be forced to sacrifice the public good to "a thousand views. . . . In a small [republic], the interest of the public is easier to perceive, better understood, and more within the reach of every citizen; abuses have a lesser extent, and of course are less protected."[12] As one of the most widely read

---

[8]Douglass G. Adair, "Experience Must Be Our Only Guide: History, Democratic Theory, and the United States Constitution," in *The Reinterpretation of the American Revolution, 1763–1789*, ed. Jack P. Greene (New York, 1968), 397–416.

[9]"Brutus," in *CA*, II: 368.

[10]"Lycurgus," *New York Daily Advertiser*, April 2, 1787, in *The Documentary History of the Ratification of the Constitution*, Vol. XIII: Commentaries on the Constitution—Public and Private, ed. John P. Kaminski and Gaspare J. Saladino (Madison, Wis., 1981), 59; "Brutus," in *CA*, II: 368; "Essay by Alfred," February 5, 1788, in *CA*, VI: 90.

[11]Charles-Louis de Secondat, Baron de Montesquieu, *The Spirit of Laws*, ed. David Wallace Carrithers and trans. Thomas Nugent (Berkeley, Calif., 1977; orig. publ. 1748), 177–79, 183–85. For examples of Antifederalist references to Montesquieu, see *CA*, II: 110, 365, 368; III: 82, 115, 190; IV: 77, 171; VI: 123, 137.

[12]Montesquieu, *Spirit of Laws*, 176.

thinkers of his time, Montesquieu was respected by both supporters and opponents of the Constitution.[13] His views had to be addressed.

The predominance of the small-republic theory in the political literature of the day narrowed the perspective of the Antifederalists, preventing them from conceiving of alternatives. They saw only what tradition taught them. Echoing Montesquieu, some Pennsylvanians insisted that nothing short of "an *iron-handed despotism* . . . could connect and govern these United States under one government."[14] "If respect is to be paid to the opinion of the greatest and wisest men who have ever thought or wrote on the science of government," said "Brutus," "we shall be constrained to conclude, that a free republic cannot succeed over a country of such immense extent."[15] The Antifederalists feared that violating the traditional wisdom would pose grave dangers to people's liberties. "A consolidated government," said "Agrippa," "is inapplicable to a great extent of country; [and] is unfriendly to the rights of both persons and property. . . . Such a government can be supported only by power."[16] Extending the republic, the Antifederalists worried, might well destroy the form of government Americans sought to pre-serve.

To further buttress their argument, the Antifederalists cited their own experience in the states. A large republic, they said, was impractical as well as undesirable. They noted that as settlers had moved into western regions, states had encountered difficulties in expanding their governments into these new areas. Westerners had protested their treatment. "Do we not already see," said "Centinel," "that the inhabitants in a number of larger states, who are remote from the seat of government, are loudly complaining of the inconveniencies and disadvantages they are subject to on this account[?]"[17] If the individual states had had problems, it would be that much more difficult to govern a republic composed of all thirteen states. As Luther Martin of Maryland saw it, "If the inhabitants of the different States consider it as a grievance to attend a *county court* or the *seat* of their *own government,* when a little inconve-

---

[13]See James H. Hutson, "Country, Court, and Constitution: Antifederalism and the Historians," *William & Mary Quarterly*, 3d ser., 38 (1981), 337–68. I disagree with Hutson's contention on page 355 that the debate over the extensive republic was "little more than a cliché of the literati of both parties."

[14]"The Address and Reasons of Dissent of the Minority of the Convention of Pennsylvania to their Constituents," *Pennsylvania Packet and Daily Advertiser*, December 18, 1787, in *CA*, III: 154.

[15]"Brutus," in *CA*, II: 368.

[16]"Agrippa," in *CA*, IV: 88.

[17]"Centinel," in *CA*, II: 141.

nient, can it be supposed they would ever *submit* to a *national government,* the seat of which would be *more than a thousand miles removed from some of them?*"[18] Drawing the obvious conclusion, "Cato" observed that "the extent of many of the states in the Union, is at this time, almost too great for the superintendence of a republican form of government."[19] Under these circumstances, then, it was nothing short of irresponsible to broaden the republic's sphere.

The practical problems of distance made an extensive republic unfair as well as unfeasible. The difficulties of travel and transportation in an extensive republic had to be taken into account. A government encompassing large distances, the Antifederalists said, caused its citizens additonal expense, burden, and inconvenience. They pointed with horror to the proposed system of federal appeals courts. Although itinerant, these bodies would still meet at large distances from many inhabitants. Justice dispensed in this manner was more than inconvenient; it was unfair to those who could least afford it. "The expence of suits," a New York "Son of Liberty" commented, "will become so enormous as to render justice unattainable but by the rich."[20] An extensive republic would favor the wealthy, who could afford to travel the long distances necessary to obtain justice.

In a similar vein, the Antifederalists opposed Article 1, Section 4, of the Constitution, which gave Congress the ultimate authority to regulate the time, place, and manner of electing congressmen. Although the states had primary responsibility for making these decisions, Congress could intervene whenever it thought it necessary. The Antifederalists seized on this possibility, insisting that Congress would routinely interfere with the states' prerogative. By manipulating the polling places, Congress could skew the election results. Its members would choose sites "where their influence [was] most extensive, and where the inhabitants [were] most obsequious to the will of their superiors"[21]—thereby guaranteeing their own reelection. Some authors imagined the most extreme possibilities: that the people of Georgia, for example, would be sent to vote in Boston or those of Maryland to vote in Georgia. Others imagined a less improbable, but still disconcerting, scenario: that Con-

---

[18]Luther Martin, "Genuine Information, Delivered to the Legislature of the State of Maryland, Relative to the Proceedings of the General Convention, Held at Philadelphia . . . ," in *CA*, II: 47–48.

[19]"Letters of Cato," *New York Journal* (1788), in *CA*, II: 111.

[20]"Objections by a Son of Liberty," *New York Journal*, November 8, 1787, in *CA*, VI: 35.

[21]"'The Government of Nature Delineated or an Exact Picture of the New Federal Constitution' by Aristocrotis" (1788), in *CA*, III: 200.

gress would establish only a single polling place for a whole state, forcing electors to travel long distances to vote.[22]

Whatever the exact plan, mass disenfranchisement of voters would result. Only those who lived near the polling places or who could afford the time and expense of traveling long distances would be able to cast their votes. Anxiety about the location of polling places was so great that every state that proposed amendments to the Constitution offered one on this subject.[23] As farfetched as these possibilities may seem today, they reflected the Antifederalists' acute awareness of the potential problems caused by large distances in an extended republic.

The Antifederalists had an additional basis for believing that a large republic would not work. They assumed a connection between extent of territory and homogeneity of population. The smaller the area, the more uniform the population was thought to be in its interests, values, and attitudes. Social uniformity was to be the basis for political unity. As one Antifederalist explained it:

> The strongest principle of union resides within our domestic walls. The ties of the parent exceed that of any other; as we depart from home, the next general principle of union is amongst citizens of the same state, where acquaintance, habits, and fortunes nourish affection, and attachment; enlarge the circle still further, and, as citizens of different states, though we acknowledge the same national denomination, we lose the ties of acquaintance, habits, and fortunes, and thus, by degrees, we lessen in our attachments, till, at length, we no more than acknowledge a sameness of species.[24]

The farther the distance, the less people had in common. The bonds of unity and affection essential to government were best sustained within small areas.

The Antifederalists maintained that in a republic a homogeneous population was not only desirable but crucial. If the nation were extremely diverse and contained too many conflicting interests, representatives would not be able to make laws appropriate for the whole community.

[22]"Essays by Republicus," *Kentucky Gazette* (Lexington), February 16, 1788, in *CA*, V: 168; "Essay by a Farmer and Planter," *Maryland Journal*, April 1, 1788, in *CA*, V: 75; "Centinel," in *CA*, II: 142. See also *CA*, IV: 42–43; IV: 189; Elliot, *Debates in the State Conventions*, III: 60; Merrill Jensen, ed., *The Documentary History of the Ratification of the Constitution*, Vol. II: Pennsylvania (Madison, Wis., 1976), 311.

[23]Jackson Turner Main, *The Antifederalists: Critics of the Constitution, 1781–1788* (New York, 1961), 151.

[24]"Cato," in *CA*, II: 112. For an interesting discussion of the bonds uniting the young republic, see Melvin Yazawa, *From Colony to Commonwealth: Familial Ideology and the Beginnings of the American Republic* (Baltimore, Md., 1985), 139–65.

"In large states the same principles of legislation will not apply to all the parts," asserted "Agrippa." "The inhabitants of warmer climates are more dissolute in their manners, and less industrious, than in colder countries. A degree of severity is, therefore, necessary with one which would cramp the spirit of the other."[25] Luther Martin of Maryland was even more pessimistic about the problems inherent in governing a disparate population. "The *different States*," he said, "composing an *extensive federal empire*, widely distant *one* from the *other*, may have *interests so totally distinct*, that the *one* part might be greatly *benefited* by what would be *destructive* to the *other*."[26] A single republic, the Antifederalists insisted, could never accommodate the variety of people, interests, morals, and manners found in the United States.

The Threat of Legislative Abuse

The Antifederalists had one final reason for opposing an extended republic—and it proved to be the most damaging of all. Effective representation, they said, could function only within a limited area. If all thirteen states were represented in a single national legislature, the representation would be unfair, inadequate, and unrepresentative, as well as prone to abuses of power.

Like most Americans up until that time, the Antifederalists espoused the concept of actual representation. Actual representation had been the prevailing mode of representation in the colonies and states until the writing of the Constitution. The concept required that the assembly mirror the structure of the larger society—that the legislators act as their constituents' mouthpieces, legislating for their expressed needs, wishes, and desires. Working out of this tradition, the Antifederalists assumed that the national legislature would conform to this pattern. "The idea that naturally suggests itself to our minds, when we speak of representatives, is, that they resemble those they represent," said Melancthon Smith at the New York ratifying convention. "They should be a true picture of the people, possess a knowledge of their circumstances and their wants, sympathize in all their distresses, and be disposed to seek their true interests."[27] Stating a similar view, dissenters from the Pennsylvania convention contended, "The representation ought to be fair, equal, and sufficiently numerous, to possess the same interests, feelings, opinions, and views which the people themselves would possess,

[25]"Agrippa," in *CA*, IV: 76.
[26]Martin, "Genuine Information . . . ," in *CA*, II: 37.
[27]Elliot, *Debates in the State Conventions*, II: 245.

were they all assembled."[28] Representation, according to the Anti-federalists, should be "real and actual," as opposed to "virtual."[29] In a literal sense, as "Brutus" noted, the representatives "are considered the sign—the people are the thing signified."[30]

For the Antifederalists, the representative assembly both reflected and contained society's diversity. But since the society encompassed only a limited area, its composition was never so diverse as to strain the legislature to the breaking point. As a microcosm of the community, the legislature reflected its class structure. Each class was to elect its "best informed men"[31] so that "the farmer, merchant, mecanick, and other various orders of people, [would] be represented according to their respective weight and numbers."[32] When it functioned properly, the legislature provided a forum that mitigated conflict among classes by providing a structured setting in which unequal groups met on equal ground. By "unit[ing] and balanc[ing]" the different classes' interests, feelings, opinions, and views, the legislature, according to the "Federal Farmer," "prevent[ed] a change in the government by the gradual exaltation of one part to the depression of others."[33] All views were represented, acknowledged, and considered.

The Antifederalists' understanding of representation presumed that effective representation could occur only within a small area, that it was inherently localistic in nature. The model for understanding the national legislature was the state assembly. The Antifederalists believed that the representatives should have a close, even intimate, knowledge of their constituents. The legislators should "know and be known by the citizens."[34] They needed to be familiar with "the common concerns and occupations of the people"[35] and to "bear a part of all the burdens they may lay upon [them]."[36] "The members of our State legislature," said "Cornelius," "are annually elected—they are subject to instructions—they are chosen within small circles—they are sent but a small distance from their respective homes: Their conduct is constantly known to their

[28]"The Address and Reasons of Dissent of the Minority of the Convention of Pennsylvania to their Constituents," *Pennsylvania Packet and Daily Advertiser*, December 18, 1787, in *CA*, III: 158.
[29]For the contemporary usage of these terms, see Elliot, *Debates in the State Conventions*, III: 31–32, 324; *CA*, IV: 181; V: 83. For a modern treatment of the concepts, see Hanna F. Pitkin, *The Concept of Representation* (Berkeley, Calif., 1967), 60–91.
[30]"Brutus," in *CA*, II: 379.
[31]"Dissent of the Pennsylvania Minority," in *CA*, III: 158.
[32]"Brutus," in *CA*, II: 380.
[33]"Federal Farmer," in *CA*, II: 268–69.
[34]"A Farmer," in *CA*, III: 184.
[35]Elliot, *Debates in the State Conventions*, II: 245.
[36]"A Farmer," in *CA*, III: 184.

constituents. They frequently see, and are seen, by the men whose servants they are."[37]

As inheritors of the Real Whig tradition, the Antifederalists insisted on their right to supervise the legislature's proceedings, personally if possible. "The confidence which the people have in their rulers, in a free republic," explained "Brutus," "arises from their knowing them, from their being responsible to them for their conduct, and from the power they have of displacing them when they misbehave."[38] If the people relaxed their vigilance, the assembly might infringe on their liberties. "The few must be watched, checked, and often resisted," warned the "Federal Farmer."[39] The threat of legislative abuse was constant. "Unless confirmed in its views and conduct," said John Francis Mercer of Maryland, "by the constant inspection, immediate superintendance, and frequent interference and control of the People themselves," representative government "is really only a scene of perpetual rapine and confusion."[40] Although not actually involved in the day-to-day legislative process, the people had an active responsibility to prevent the legislature from abusing its power.

The tenets of actual representation provided the Antifederalists with abundant ammunition to use against the Constitution. For one, the new national legislature would not reflect the composition of the whole country. And there would be far too few representatives for far too many people. Dissenters from the Pennsylvania ratifying convention scoffed that, "The sense and views of 3 or 4 millions of people diffused over so extensive a territory comprising such various climates, products, habits, interests, and opinions, cannot [possibly] be collected in so small a body."[41] The representatives would not know or be known by the people. Because thirty thousand or more people would elect each representative, the congressmen could not have sufficient familiarity with their constituents to be able to legislate for them. They would not, the "Federal Farmer" said, "be well informed as to the circumstances of the people, the member of it must be too far removed from the people, in general, to sympathize with them, and too few to communicate with them."[42] "Cornelius" explicitly and negatively contrasted federal representatives with state legislators. "The members of Congress," he said, "are to be chosen for a term of years. They are to be subject to no

[37] "Cornelius," in *CA*, IV: 141.
[38] "Brutus," in *CA*, II: 370–71.
[39] "Federal Farmer," in *CA*, II: 274.
[40] "Address by John Francis Mercer to the Members of the Conventions of New York and Virginia," April or May 1788, in *CA*, V: 105.
[41] "Dissent of the Pennsylvania Minority," in *CA*, III: 158.
[42] "Federal Farmer," in *CA*, II: 268.

instructions. They are to be chosen within large circles: they will be unknown to a very considerable part of their constituents, and their constituents will be not less unknown to them."[43]

If federal representatives could hardly be acquainted with their own constituents, they would know even less about the rest of the country. "Will the man of Georgia," asked James Monroe, "possess sufficient information to legislate for the local concerns of New-Hampshire? Or of New-Hampshire for those of Georgia? Or contract it to a smaller space[,] of New-York for those of Virginia? Will not of course most of its measures be taken upon an imperfect view of the subject?"[44] Such a small body of men representing such a vast and varied population could not possibly be responsive to the people's wishes. In disgust, a "Republican Federalist" concluded, "We might as well have committed ourselves to the Parliament of Great–Britain, under the idea of *virtual representation* as in this manner resign ourselves to the federal government."[45]

The Antifederalists also claimed that Congress would be unrepresentative of the social divisions within the larger society. Those elected would come primarily from the upper ranks. Only men who occupied a "high and exalted" position would have the financial means, reputation, and influence to be elected to the few available seats. Few farmers or mechanics would be sent to Congress. As a result, said Samuel Chase of Maryland, the national legislature "will be ignorant of the sentiments of the middling *and much more of the lower* class of citizens, strangers to their ability, unacquainted with their wants, difficulties and distress and need of sympathy and fellow feeling."[46] Ordinary people would feel alienated from the more aristocratic representatives. Congress, "Brutus" noted, "will not be viewed by the people as part of themselves, but as a body distinct from them, and having separate interests to pursue."[47] Rather than mitigating conflict among the classes, the new national legislature would accentuate it.

Finally, the Antifederalists maintained that the new system would prevent citizens from adequately supervising their legislature, hence creating an environment unsafe for the people's liberties. The large distances between the people and their legislators, and the lack of communication between them, would encourage congressmen to ignore

[43]"Cornelius," in *CA*, IV: 141.
[44]"From the Debates in the Virginia ratifying convention," in *CA*, V: 287.
[45]"Letters of a Republican Federalist," *Massachusetts Centinel*, January 1788, in *CA*, IV: 181.
[46]Samuel Chase, "Notes of Speeches Delivered to the Maryland Ratifying Convention," April 1788, in *CA*, V: 90. See also *CA* II: 381; Elliot, *Debates in the State Conventions*, II: 245.
[47]"Brutus," in *CA*, II: 385.

their constituents' interests. Separation, said "John DeWitt," would make the representatives "strangers to the very people choosing them."[48] Residents in some parts of the country would live over a thousand miles from the nation's seat of government. At such a far remove, the people would have no immediate means of stopping the legislature from abusing its power. Some New York citizens cited three related objections to the proposed government: "the extensive territory of the United States, the dispersed situation of its inhabitants, and the insuperable difficulty of controuling or counteracting the views of a set of men (however unconstitutional and oppressive their acts might be)."[49] "Cornelius" pointed out the dangers inherent in the situation. "They will be far removed, and long detained from the view of their constituents," he said. "Their general conduct will be unknown. Their chief connections will be with men of the first rank in the United States, who have been bred in affluence at least, if not in the excess of luxury."[50] Large distances in the new nation would prevent the people from exercising the vigilance necessary to guarantee freedom. To adopt such a system would be dangerous as well as unwise.

Like most other Americans until that time, the Antifederalists fully accepted the dictates of actual representation and had expected the new government to conform to its strictures. Their concept of representation constrained the size of republican government to a relatively small area. The need for personal contact between representatives and constituents, the importance of supervising the legislature's actions, and the desirability of keeping the legislators responsive to citizens' needs all constricted the sphere in which republican government could effectively operate. The Antifederalist idea of government was localistic in nature, incapable of extension to a large territory.[51]

From this perspective, then, an extensive republic seemed like a contradiction in terms—"like a house," said "Cato," "divided against itself."[52] The Antifederalists simply could not conceive of a form of representation that would be suitable for such a large area. As *Federalist* No. 27 indicated, they could not envision how a government "at a

[48]"Essays of John DeWitt," *American Herald* (Boston), 1787, in *CA*, IV: 28.

[49]Robert Yates and John Lansing, Jr., to the Governor of New York, in *The Records of the Federal Convention of 1787*, ed. Max Farrand (New Haven, Conn., 1911), III: 246.

[50]"Cornelius," in *CA*, IV: 141.

[51]Contrary to what historian Cecelia Kenyon argues, it was not a lack of faith in human nature but a system of representation incapable of extension to larger areas that prevented the Antifederalists from assenting to the Constitution. Still, her discussion of the Antifederalists remains seminal. See her "Men of Little Faith: The Anti-Federalists on the Nature of Representative Government," in Greene, *Reinterpretation of the American Revolution*, 526–66.

[52]"Cato," in *CA*, II: 110.

tance and out of sight"[53] would remain sensitive to the people's needs and wishes as well as stay above the suspicion of corruption. As a group, they simply could not move beyond their traditional spatial assumptions about representation.

The Federalist Response

The arguments against an extended republic attacked the very premise underlying the Constitution. Supporters of the document realized that history, political theory, and experience all gave credence to the Antifederalist view. The burden of proof that the new system could work rested with the Federalists. If they did not decisively discredit their opponents' ideas, they would risk losing the whole debate. As a result, they mounted a two-pronged assault: to undermine the spatial assumptions behind the small-republic theory and to present a viable alternative to actual representation.

One Federalist tactic was simply to deny that distances would pose problems in the new republic. The Federalists claimed that their opponents were imagining that the situation would be much worse than it was. "There is in most of the arguments which relate to distance," said Alexander Hamilton in *Federalist* No. 84, "a palpable illusion of the imagination."[54] Most Americans, the Federalists contended, would not have to travel long distances to attend federal appellate sessions. Even for those who did, distance would prove to be no burden to the just man. If an individual had a winning case, said one Federalist, "the man in low circumstances would have nothing to fear, as the payment of all charges would fall upon the person who lost the cause."[55] In regard to Congress's altering the polling places for the election of congressmen, the Federalists denied that the federal legislature would interfere at all, unless the states overreached their powers.[56]

More generally, the Federalists insisted that once the new government was formed, distances would be more easily overcome. In *Federalist* No. 14, James Madison insisted that "intercourse through the union

[53]Hamilton, Jay, and Madison, *The Federalist*, 173. The phrase is Hamilton's, but it accurately describes the Antifederalist perception of the proposed government.

[54]Ibid., 582.

[55]"Cassius," *Massachusetts Gazette*, December 21, 1787, in *Essays on the Constitution of the United States*, ed. Paul Leicester Ford (New York, 1892), 40.

[56]Pennsylvania Ratifying Convention, November 28, 1787, in Jensen, *Ratification of the Constitution*, II: 402–3.

will be daily facilitated by new improvements," such as more roads, new canals, and better accommodations for travelers.[57] In *Federalist* No. 84, Hamilton argued that distance would not result in Congress's infringing on the people's rights. "Impediments to a prompt communication which distance may be supposed to create," he said, "will be overballanced by the effects of vigilance of the state governments."[58] The Federalists' point was that practical problems should not deter Americans from accepting the Constitution. The passage of time and the new government's greater energy would overcome these problems. What the Federalists ignored, however, was that the Constitution would take effect long before the roads were improved and the canals built. Their arguments did little to ease their opponents' fears in the present time.

The Federalists also did not have a conclusive rejoinder to the Antifederalists' charge that the new country was too diverse to be governed as a single republic. Where their opponents saw heterogeneity, they claimed to see common threads such as Protestantism, the English legal tradition, and the English language. "From New Hampshire to Georgia," asserted Hamilton, "the people of America are as uniform in their interests and manners as those of any [country] established in Europe."[59] Whatever social unity the country lacked could be imposed by the new government. "The proposed system," wrote John Adams, "seems admirably calculated to unite [the people's] interests and affections and bring them to an uniformity of principles."[60] The new government's greater energy and superior administration would diminish citizens' localistic tendencies and encourage a wider loyalty. Under the Constitution, said "A Freeman," Americans would "give up local attachments, and . . . cement together as *one great people,* pursuing one general interest."[61] Social unity would emerge from a firm basis of political unity. In retrospect, the Federalists appear prescient; but at the time, national unity was by no means foreordained. The Antifederalists, then, regarded such ideas as so much wishful thinking.

The Federalists made a somewhat more persuasive, but still less than completely convincing, argument in response to the Antifederalists' invocation of history and political theory. Supporters of the Constitution

[57]Hamilton, Jay, and Madison, *The Federalist*, 86–87.
[58]Ibid., 582.
[59]Elliot, *Debates in the State Conventions*, II: 267.
[60]Hon. John Adams to Col. Smith, December 26, 1787, in *The Maryland Gazette; or, the Baltimore Advertiser,* April 15, 1788.
[61]"A Freeman: To the People of Connecticut," *Connecticut Courant,* December 31, 1787, in *The Documentary History of the Ratification of the Constitution,* Vol. III: Delaware, New Jersey, Georgia and Connecticut, ed. Merrill Jensen (Madison, 1978), 518.

tried to show that traditional theories did not apply to the United States, that the country's situation was unprecedented. Arguments against an extended republic, they said, "were laid down before the science of government was as well understood as it is now."[62] Montesquieu, observed "Cato," had been "born and educated under a monarchical government and knew nothing of any other but in theory."[63] The traditional theories had in fact already been discredited by the continuing existence of the state governments. According to the Federalists, most of the states were larger than the optimum size recommended for republics—yet all still had flourishing republican governments. "When Montesquieu recommends a small extent for republics," noted Hamilton in *Federalist* No. 9, "the standards he had in view were of dimensions, far short of the limits of almost every one of these States."[64] If Montesquieu had been correct, said a delegate to the Virginia ratifying convention, his objections would apply "against this and every State in the Union, except Delaware and Rhode Island."[65] In short, Americans simply should not take seriously "the old worn-out idea that republican government is best calculated for a small territory."[66]

Yet all of these responses answered the Antifederalists in their own terms. As long as the Antifederalists established the framework of the debate, the Federalists would be on the defensive. The only way for them to make real headway against their opponents was to attack the assumptions underlying the Antifederalists' claims, to undermine their belief that space somehow limited the compass of republican government.

To this end, the Federalists assailed the claim that a community's physical size determined the homogeneity of its population. A uniform society such as the one the Antifederalists described would never experience dissent, because, as Madison put it in a letter to Jefferson, "the interest of the majority would be that of the minority also."[67] Citizens would always agree on what was best for the community. Yet, as Madison declared to Jefferson, "We know that no Society ever did or can consist of so homogeneous a mass of Citizens."[68] A small republic, according to the Federalists, was no more likely than a larger one to support a population with uniform values and interests. If the Anti-

[62]Elliot, *Debates in the State Conventions*, III: 199.
[63]"Cato," *Country Journal, & Poughkeepsie Advertiser*, December 12, 1787.
[64]Hamilton, Jay, and Madison, *The Federalist*, 52–53.
[65]Elliot, *Debates in the State Conventions*, III: 108.
[66]Ibid., III: 107.
[67]James Madison to Thomas Jefferson, October 24, 1787, in *The Papers of Thomas Jefferson*, ed. Julian P. Boyd (Princeton, N.J., 1951–), XII: 276–77.
[68]Ibid.

federalists desired a small republic because they hoped to ensure an identity of interests among its citizens, their desire was based on a myth.

The Federalists also pointed out that small size did not guarantee internal stability. Small republics were, if anything, more susceptible than larger ones to the tumult produced by factionalism. Factions pursued their own narrow interests at the expense of the common good. In all republics, a faction composed of a minority could be outvoted and hence put down. But, as Madison noted in *Federalist* No. 10, in a small community a majority faction was virtually unstoppable.[69] No countervailing force could prevent it from having its way. The Federalists cited examples. "The ancient democracies," contended Hamilton, "never possessed one feature of good government. Their very character was tyranny; their figure, deformity."[70] The smallest state in the Union was also the most troubled. Charles Pinckney reminded the South Carolina ratifying convention that in Rhode Island licentiousness prevailed to such an extent "as to seize the reins of government, and oppress the people by laws the most infamous that have ever disgraced a civilized nation."[71] If the Antifederalists hoped to avoid internal upheaval by keeping the republic small, they were deluding themselves.

The Federalists proceeded to explain how a republic could, in fact, succeed in a territory of any size. They contrasted a democracy and a republic. In a direct democracy, because all electors participated directly in the law-making process, the government could exist only in a relatively small area. If it encompassed too much territory and too many people, it would never be able to accomplish anything. Under a republican form of government, however, only the people's representatives—not all the people themselves—attended meetings of the legislature. As a result, a republic could accommodate a much larger territory than a democracy. A "remedy" to the "evil" of large size "has long since been found out," said the Federalist "Cato." "When the territory of any state became too large for the general assembling of the people, it was thought best to transact the business of the Commonwealth by representation."[72]

Indeed, republics seemed peculiarly suited for large areas. The primary constraint on a republic's size, Madison argued, was the representatives' ability to travel to meetings of the legislature. "The natural limit of a republic," he remarked in *Federalist* No. 14, "is that distance from

[69]Hamilton, Jay, and Madison, *The Federalist*, 60–1.
[70]Elliot, *Debates in the State Conventions*, II: 253–54.
[71]Ibid., IV: 327.
[72]"Cato," *Country Journal, & Poughkeepsie Advertiser*, December 12, 1787. In *Federalist* No. 10, Madison, of course, makes the classic statement on this point.

the center, which will barely allow the representatives of the people to meet as often as may be necessary for the adminstration of public affairs."[73] Such a limit was very large indeed, even given the difficulties of transportation in the eighteenth century. Some even claimed that the theoretical extent of a republic was unlimited. "If," said Edmund Randolph, "the business of legislation be transacted by representatives, chosen periodically by the people, it is obvious that it may be done in any extent of country."[74] Physical size, the Federalists suggested, was ultimately irrelevant in a republic.

Pursuing their analysis of the role of size even further, the Federalists insisted that a large republic was not only possible but preferable.[75] Whereas factional majorities had plagued and disrupted smaller republics, the very extent of territory in a large republic would mitigate their effect, thus removing one of the primary threats to a republic's stability.[76] A large territory could defeat majority factions through a variety of means. For one, a large republic would be more likely to have a wide diversity of interests and parties, which would make it unlikely that one faction would be able to persuade a large number of people to join its cause. As Charles Pinckney observed, when "the sphere of government [will be] enlarged, it will not easily be in the power of factious and designing men to infect the whole people; it will give an opportunity to the more temperate and prudent part of the society to correct the licentiousness and injustice of the rest."[77] The more people there were, the more likely that they would have different, if not conflicting, interests. In his 1787 essay, "The Vices of the Political System," Madison put it this way:

> If an enlargement of the sphere is found to lessen the insecurity of private rights, it is . . . because a common interest or passion is less apt to be felt and the requisite combinations less easy to be formed by a great than by a small number. The Society becomes broken into a greater variety of interests, of pursuits, of passions, which check each other, whilst those who may feel a common sentiment have less opportunity of communication and concert.[78]

[73]Hamilton, Jay, and Madison, *The Federalist*, 85. I believe that historian Garry Wills underestimates the importance of space in preventing the formation of factious majorities in his *Explaining America* (New York, 1981), 220.

[74]Elliot, *Debates in the State Conventions*, III: 199.

[75]Douglass G. Adair argues persuasively that they borrowed the idea from David Hume, in his "That Politics May Be Reduced to a Science: David Hume, James Madison, and the Tenth 'Federalist,'" in Greene, *Reinterpretation of the American Revolution*, 487–503.

[76]Hamilton, Jay, and Madison, *The Federalist*, 62–65.

[77]Elliot, *Debates in the State Conventions*, IV: 327.

[78]Robert A. Rutland, ed., *The Papers of James Madison* (Chicago, 1956–1979), IX: 356–57.

Since many more people would be required to constitute a majority faction in a large republic, the likelihood of convincing enough people to unite, in what Madison called in *Federalist* No. 10, "unjust or dishonorable purposes," would be substantially lessened.[79]

In addition, the difficulties of transportation and communication, which the Antifederalists saw as a liability, became an asset in the Federalists' republic. It would prevent those with selfish intentions from uniting with those of like mind. An extensive territory, suggested Pinckney, "will not permit them all to be assembled at one time and in one place."[80] Those with factional intentions were less likely to be aware of others with similar intentions. "The people in such distant parts," remarked Gouverneur Morris at the federal Convention, "can not communicate & act in concert."[81] As a result, according to John Dickinson, "THE EXTENT of our territory, and the NUMBER of states within it, vastly increase the difficulty of any political order diffusing its contagion."[82] The physical size of the republic, the sheer numbers of people involved, and the diversity of their interests would all make the formation of factious majorities difficult, if not impossible. An extended republic, then, was superior to one limited in area.

Representation in the Extensive Republic

Having refuted the spatial assumptions behind the small-republic theory, the Federalists had to explain how an extensive republic would function, especially in the realm of representation. Of all the Antifederalists' arguments against an extended republic, the actual-representation argument was in many ways the most difficult to answer. The Federalists could not simply deny its validity; Americans had been accustomed to it since colonial days. They could not simply modify its basic tenets, because it was, by definition, inapplicable to large areas. As a result, they had to construct a new concept of representation, one that did not depend on physical proximity for its efficacy.

Some Federalists argued that their opponents had overstated the prevalence of actual representation in the country. Few, if any, states, they said, elected representatives from all classes of society in proportion to their numbers. One Federalist viewed the prospect with horror: "God

---

[79]Hamilton, Jay, and Madison, *The Federalist*, 64.

[80]Elliot, *Debates in the State Conventions*, IV: 327.

[81]James Madison, *Notes of Debates in the Federal Convention of 1787*, ed. Adrienne Koch (New York, 1966), 235.

[82]John Dickinson, *Letters of Fabius* (Wilmington, Del., 1797), 60.

knows what fools and knaves have voice enough in government already; it is to be hoped these wise prophesiers of evil would not wish to give them a constitutional privilege to send members in proportion to their numbers."[83] Hamilton dismissed the notion of actual representation as "altogether visionary."[84] In *Federalist* No. 35, he argued that, in fact, people always tended to elect their betters to the legislature in the knowledge that their interests could "be more effectually promoted" by the elite than by members of their own class. "Mechanics and manufacturers," he said, "will always be inclined with few exceptions to give their votes to merchants in preference to persons of their own professions or trades."[85] To demand that Congress reflect society's exact composition even when the state legislatures did not was, in the Federalists' opinion, ludicrous.

Despite occasional lapses into the rhetoric of actual representation,[86] the Federalists by and large rejected the view that the national legislature should mirror the people's wishes, needs, and desires. Rather than representing all ranks of society, legislators elected to the Congress were to be among the wisest and most virtuous men in society—men who knew, and would act on, the public good. In a large republic, suggested Madison in *Federalist* No. 10, the most competent men were more likely to be chosen. As he saw it, a greater number of suitable candidates would emerge from the larger field of available contenders. Equally important, a larger number of voters would be more likely to elect the best men to office. Whereas a small group of citizens might be deceived by a candidate's behavior or reputation, a larger group would be better able to discern the truth. It would, according to Madison, "be more difficult for unworthy candidates to practice with success the vicious arts, by which elections are too often carried."[87] The individuals who were elected, then, would be in the Federalists' words, "discerning and intelligent,"[88] as well as "of approved probity and talents."[89] Unlike the

---

[83] "Cato," *Country Journal, & Poughkeepsie Advertiser*, December 12, 1787.

[84] Hamilton, Jay, and Madison, *The Federalist*, 219.

[85] Ibid.

[86] As late as the Pennsylvania ratifying convention, James Wilson said that an assembly "ought to be the most exact transcript of the whole society." Doubtless other, similar expressions could be traced to the Federalists. Nevertheless, the whole thrust of their thinking, as it developed from the federal Convention through the ratification debates, was a move away from actual representation. Quote from Pitkin, *Concept of Representation*, 60–61. I obviously disagree with James Hutson's suggestion, in "Country, Court, and Constitution," p. 355, that "the Federalist theory of representation seems identical to . . . the Antifederalist theory." I see a fundamental divergence between the two views.

[87] Hamilton, Jay, and Madison, *The Federalist*, 63.

[88] Elliot, *Debates in the State Conventions*, II: 265–66.

[89] *New-York Packet*, July 11, 1788.

Antifederalists, who wanted to elect even common men to Congress, the Federalists explicitly favored the election of an elite. Though they preferred a "natural aristocracy" of talent over one determined by wealth and family connections, they still wanted the best and the brightest to govern.[90]

The Federalists also claimed that federal representatives had a different function than state legislators. Rather than being spokesmen for local interests, these representatives were to be adjudicators of the common good. In a country whose interests were so diverse, the congressmen were to sort out competing claims and determine what was best for the nation. As a "Republican" put it, they should be "men who know what the public good requires; and have the virtue to act accordingly."[91] Federal representatives should remain aloof from the people's momentary passions, yet be sensitive to their long-term best interests. "I would not have the first wish, the momentary impulse of the public mind, become law," said Fisher Ames at the Massachusetts ratifying convention. "For it is not always the sense of the people with whom I admit all power resides. . . . The representation of the people, is something more than the people."[92] Despite the fact that citizens from a particular district or state elected them, congressmen represented the interests of all Americans. Raising themselves above the fray, these men alone would determine what was best for the nation.

Because the scope of the national government was more general than that of the states, federal representatives did not need to have as close a relationship with their constituents as did state legislators. They did not need to know, and be known by, their constituents in a personal way. Furthermore, a good understanding of the national interest did not require a detailed knowledge of all states—or even of one's own state. "A particular knowledge," said Hamilton, " . . . of the local circumstances of any state, as they may vary in different districts, is unnecessary for the federal representative. As he is not to represent the interests or local wants of the county of Duchess or Montgomery, neither is it necessary that he should be acquainted with their particular resources."[93] Even one of Congress's most important powers, the right to tax, did not

[90]See Gordon S. Wood's discussion of the Federalists in *The Creation of the American Republic, 1776–1787* (New York, 1969), esp. 506–18.

[91]"The Republican: To the People," *Connecticut Courant*, January 7, 1788, in Jensen, *Ratification of the Constitution*, III: 532.

[92]*Debates and Proceedings in the Convention of the Commonwealth of Massachusetts, Held in the Year 1788, and Which Finally Ratified the Constitution of the United States* (Boston, 1856), 105, 107.

[93]Elliot, *Debates in the State Conventions*, II: 265–66.

depend on the legislators' specific knowledge of local circumstances. "A skillful individual in his closet," said Madison in *Federalist* No. 56, "with all the local codes before him, might compile a law on some subjects of taxation for the whole union, without any aid from oral information."[94] Unlike the bond between the people and their state legislators, the link between voters and their congressmen was not intended to be intimate.

The people, moreover, were supposed to play a more passive role in the new government. They had no duty to instruct the congressmen on their wishes or to provide personal supervision of the legislature. As a result, federal representation was not restricted by the need for the physical proximity of representatives and constituents. Hence, government could more easily be extended over a wide area.

This new conception of representation allowed the Federalists to dismiss the charge that the new legislature was too small to represent the whole country. According to Madison, the only guidelines regarding a legislature's size were that "a certain number at least seems to be necessary to secure the benefits of free consultation and discussion, and to guard against too easy a combination for improper purposes: As, on the other hand, the number ought to be kept within a certain limit, in order to avoid the confusion and intemperance of a multitude."[95] The state assemblies, said the Federalists, varied widely in size, ranging from sixty-five to three hundred.[96] Because federal representatives did not need to have a personal knowledge of their constituents, one person could adequately represent thirty thousand in the lower house—and sixty-five would adequately represent the nation.

Furthermore, the fact that representation would be proportional to population in the lower house meant that the United States would avoid the worst abuses of the English system. "No decayed and venal borough will have an *unjust* share in their determination," said "An American Citizen." "No old Sarum will send thither a representative *by the voice of a single elector*."[97] Given the Federalists' new conception of the representative's role, Congress was sufficiently large to handle its tasks. If the representation was sound, moreover, then the exact size of the legislature need not be a matter of great concern.

The Federalists' theory of representation represented a radical innovation. Rejecting the "old, worn-out" ideas about representation,[98] the

[94]Hamilton, Jay, and Madison, *The Federalist*, 380.
[95]Ibid., 374.
[96]Ibid., 373; Elliot, *Debates in the State Conventions*, II: 238.
[97]"An American Citizen," "On the Federal Government," *New-York Packet*, October 16, 1787.
[98]Elliot, *Debates in the State Conventions*, III: 107.

Federalists took extensiveness as their starting point and constructed a theory that could accommodate this fact of American life. In order to refute the Antifederalists' arguments, they changed the terms of the debate. They not only challenged the old spatial assumptions about representation but articulated a new idea of representation—one that depended on the quality of representation itself, not on the physical proximity of representatives and constituents. Like the English version of virtual representation, the Federalist version of representation could cover a country of any size. Unlike the English version, however, the Federalist version of representation would give the majority of people a true stake in the system.

At bottom, the Federalists and Antifederalists had fundamentally different ideas about the function of the national legislature. Although both believed that representatives should legislate for the common good, they disagreed as to how the common good was determined. The Antifederalists maintained that each class and interest group should be represented in the assembly. The representatives should know their constituents personally and be intimately familiar with their needs and wishes. If each faction were properly represented, legislators could discuss their differences and enact laws that could accommodate all the members of society. The Antifederalists complained that they wanted "a more *feeling* representation in the lower house."[99] A New York Federalist was baffled by that kind of thinking. "As to the idea of representing the feelings of the people," he said, "I do not entirely understand it, unless by their feelings are meant their interests. . . . If [the people] have feelings which do not rise out of their interests, I think they ought not to be represented. What, shall the unjust, the selfish, the unsocial feelings, be represented?"[100] Unlike the Antifederalists, the Federalists believed that the determination of the common good resulted from a reasoned consultation among the wise and virtuous rather than being an automatic reflection of society's interests. They claimed that a national legislature should not and could not possibly respond to localistic demands. Rather, it was up to the representatives to determine what was in the national interest. To do so, federal legislators needed the virtue, wisdom, and integrity that would enable them to make hard decisions.

The New Ideal

The Federalists changed forever Americans' perception of the relationship between space and representation, at least at the national level.

[99]"William Symmes," in *CA*, IV: 63.
[100]Elliot, *Debates in the State Conventions*, II: 275–76.

In justifying an extended republic, supporters of the Constitution had undermined the prevailing spatial assumptions about representation— by challenging the need for proximity to the seat of government, for a personal supervision of the legislature, and for a close relationship between representatives and constituents. Although it took many years for actual representation to loosen its grip on the American imagination and for Federalist notions to gain complete acceptance, the Federalists had given Americans a new framework for understanding representation—a framework that did not depend on distance, size, or territory for its efficacy.

Yet, even after the new government went into operation, some still feared that the old theories would prove to be true. A few years after the Constitution's ratification, the editors of the *Universal Asylum, and Columbian Magazine* ran an article designed to demonstrate "the Fallacy of the Polical Doctrine, that Civil Liberty can only exist in a Small Territory." They commented, "There is probably no opinion of Montesquieu, from the refutation of which so much satisfaction would arise in the minds of the citizens of the United States. It is true," they continued, that Americans "have, at this moment, an experimental proof of its fallacy; but it is to be feared, notwithstanding, that *some* are apprehensive lest this should not continue, without any better reason for their fears than Montesquieu's opinion."[101] Despite the Federalists' ultimate triumph, spatial assumptions about representation died hard.

[101] "On the Fallacy of the Political Doctrine, That Civil Liberty Can Only Exist in a Small Territory," *Universal Asylum, and Columbian Magazine* (March 1791), 144.

CHAPTER 5

Creating Congressional Constituencies

After ratifying the federal Constitution, the states faced the task of implementing it. Among the powers delegated to the states was that of regulating "the Times, Places and Manner of holding elections for Senators and Representatives." According to Article 1, Section 4, the states retained the authority to establish their own polling places, election days, suffrage requirements, and, most importantly, procedures by which congressmen would be elected to the House of Representatives. Within and among the states, the method of electing federal representatives soon became a matter of intense dispute over exactly what the new Constitution meant.

Most legislators saw the problem as a choice between two alternatives: at-large or district elections. Under the at-large, or general-ticket, system, as it was called, all the voters in a state would vote for all of the state's congressmen.[1] Connecticut, for example, had six congressmen; each resident therefore voted for six candidates, who, if elected, would represent the entire state. The district method, by contrast, divided the state into as many districts as it had congressmen. Each voter would vote for only one representative, who would represent his district. Although both systems were permissible under the language of the Constitution, each implied a different definition of whom and what a congressman represented.

---

[1] The term *at-large* will be used here as a synonym for general-ticket elections. After the Civil War, however, *at-large* took on a different meaning, referring to states that elected most of their congressmen by districts but that allowed one or two representatives to be elected by the whole state.

By the mid-1790s, most states had settled on one method or the other. Yet, as in previous decisions about representative institutions, state size proved to be a crucial factor in determining which method was selected. Legislators in the small states chose the general-ticket system; those in the large states selected the district system.

The Emerging Debate

Delegates to the federal Constitutional Convention had left the method of electing congressmen up to the legislators in each state. At the Convention, the delegates had not addressed the question in any detail. Most of those who spoke on the subject seemed to believe that the state legislators could best decide what plan was most suitable for their constituents.[2] James Madison expressed the general view: "Whether the electors should vote by ballot or viva voce, should assemble at this place or that place; should be divided into districts or all meet at one place, shd. all vote for all the representatives; or all in a district vote for a number allotted to the district; these & many other points would depend on the Legislatures."[3] In the end, the Constitution was deliberately vague as to the proper manner of electing federal representatives.

During the ratification debates, the mode of electing congressmen failed to become a significant point of contention between supporters and opponents of the Constitution. When they addressed the subject at all, both the Federalists and the Antifederalists tended to favor the district system. According to the Antifederalists' most eloquent spokesman, the "Federal Farmer," district elections were necessary "to render tolerably equal and secure the federal representation."[4] The Antifederalists feared that states using the at-large method would establish only one polling place. If this situation occurred, "Brutus" warned, "the representatives of the state may be elected by one tenth part of the people who actually vote."[5] In a similar vein, Melancthon Smith of New York worried that the at-large system might result in all the representatives being drawn "from a small part of the state, and the bulk of the

---

[2]Charles C. Pinckney of South Carolina did speak out in favor of districting. See James Madison, *Notes of Debates in the Federal Convention of 1787*, ed. Adrienne Koch (New York, 1966), 166, 375.

[3]Ibid., 424.

[4]"Letters from the Federal Farmer," in *The Complete Anti-Federalist*, ed. Herbert J. Storing, with the editorial assistance of Murray Dry (Chicago, 1981), II: 298 (hereafter cited as *CA*).

[5]"Brutus," in *CA*, II: 386.

people, therefore might not be fully represented."[6] At the New York ratifying convention, Smith actually proposed a constitutional amendment that would require that each state be divided into districts.[7]

The Federalists made claims similar to those of the Antifederalists. Many, in fact, presumed that the district system would prevail. Rufus King, for example, mentioned that Massachusetts would be "thrown into eight *districts,* and a member apportioned to each."[8] In South Carolina, Charles C. Pinckney maintained, "There will be no necessity . . . for all the freeholders in the state to meet at Charleston to choose five members for the House of Representatives; for the state may be divided into five election districts, and the freeholders in each election district may choose one representative."[9] Madison pointed out the advantages of the district system in *Federalist* No. 56. If the largest state were split into ten or twelve districts, he said, "it will be found that there will be no peculiar local interest in either, which will not be within the knowledge of the representative of the district."[10] Both sides seemed to agree that the district system represented the preferred method of electing congressmen.

After ratification, however, the consensus disappeared. Politicians began to realize that the method used to elect congressmen would play a large part in determining who was ultimately elected.[11] Realizing the potential for manipulation that this choice opened to the legislature, Patrick Henry commented, "The power over the manner [of election] admits of the most dangerous latitude."[12] Nevertheless, after some experimentation during the first federal elections, most of the original thirteen states had, by the second round of elections, settled into the plan they would continue to use until 1842, when Congress passed a law requiring district elections.

As state legislators made their choices, a difference became apparent

[6]Jonathan Elliot, ed., *The Debates in the Several State Conventions, on the Adoption of the Federal Constitution* . . . (Washington, D.C., 1937), II: 327.

[7]Ibid.

[8]Ibid., II: 50.

[9]Ibid., IV: 302.

[10]Alexander Hamilton, John Jay, and James Madison, *The Federalist,* ed. Jacob E. Cooke (Middletown, Conn., 1961; orig. publ. 1788), 380.

[11]"It must occur to you," wrote Pennsylvanian Thomas Fitzsimmons to Samuel Meredith in 1788, "that the representation of this state in the new Congress will in a great measure depend upon the plan that may be adopted for choosing them." Fitzsimmons to Meredith, August 20, 1788, in *The Documentary History of the First Federal Elections, 1788–1790,* ed. Merrill Jensen and Robert A. Becker (Madison, Wis., 1976), I: 253 (hereafter cited as *First Federal Elections*).

[12]Elliot, *Debates in the State Conventions,* III: 175.

between the states choosing the district system and those implementing the general-ticket method. There was a strong continuity from the small-state alliance at the federal Convention to the states choosing at-large elections. By 1791, Connecticut, New Jersey, Delaware, Rhode Island, New Hampshire, and Georgia had settled on the at-large method. The first three of these states had belonged to the small-state coalition in Philadelphia. Although neither Rhode Island nor New Hampshire had participated in the debate over representation in 1787, their small areas and populations clearly linked them with the smaller states. Only Georgia, which had sided with the large states at the Convention, now switched allegiance.

In contrast, large states tended to hold district elections for congressmen. Massachusetts, Pennsylvania, Virginia, North Carolina, South Carolina, New York, and Maryland selected district plans. Not coincidentally, the first four of these states had been allied as large states at the federal Convention. New York, which had always been an anomaly in the small-state coalition and which had a large area and population, now joined the other large states. Only Maryland defected from the small-state to the large-state ranks.[13] (See appendix 4.)

Delegates from the different states had sound reasons for their decisions. Districts appeared to be unnecessary in the small states. Since

[13] "An Act for Regulating the Election of Senators and Representatives, for This State, in the Congress of the United States," *New-Haven Gazette and Connecticut Magazine*, October 23, 1788; "An Act for Carrying into Effect, on the Part of the State of New-Jersey, the Constitution of the United States, Assented to, Ratified and Confirmed by This State on the Eighteenth Day of December, in the Year of Our Lord One Thousand Seven Hundred and Eighty Seven," *New-Jersey Journal and Political Intelligencer* (Elizabethtown), December 8, 1788; "An Act Prescribing the Times, Manner and Places for Holding Elections for Members to Represent This State, in the Congress of the United States," December 24, 1791, in *Georgia Session Laws* (Augusta, 1792), 36; "An Act for Dividing the Commonwealth into Districts for the Choice of Representatives in the Congress of the United States, and Prescribing the Mode of Election," November 19, 1788, in *Resolves of the General Court of the Commonwealth of Massachusetts* (Boston, 1788), 53; "An Act to Provide for the Election of Representatives of the People of This State in the Congress of the United States," March 16, 1791, in *Acts of the General Assembly of the Commonwealth of Pennsylvania* (Philadelphia, 1791), 15–17; "An Act for the Election of Representatives Pursuant to the Constitution of Government of the United States," November 20, 1788, in *The Statutes at Large: Being a Collection of All the Laws of Virginia, from the First Session of the Legislature in the Year 1619*, comp. William Waller Hening (Richmond, 1823), XII: 653–55; "An Act Directing the Manner of Electing Representatives to Represent This State in Congress," November 1789, in *Laws of the State of North Carolina*, comp. James Iredell (Edenton, 1791), 661–62; "An Act Directing the Times, Places and Manner of Electing Representatives in This State [New York] for the House of Representatives of the Congress of the United States of America," January 28, 1789, in Library of Congress, Rare Book room, Broadside Collection 116, no. 16r; "A Supplement to the Act, Entitled, 'An Act Directing the Time, Places and Manner, of Holding Elections for Representatives of

these states covered relatively confined areas without large differences in values, climate, or economic interests, their populations tended to be more homogeneous than those in the larger states. A representative could know and represent an entire state. A Connecticut resident pointed out in 1791 that his state's "compactness, its geographical uniformity, the simplicity of its interests, and the universal and equal distribution of population, wealth, conditions, [and] possessions" made it "the last of all states, which an advocate for district election would select for an experiment."[14] A senator from New Hampshire once remarked that districts might be useful in the large states "but not [in] the small ones, in which every man proposed to their suffrage, by general ticket, was almost equally well known to his constituents, as if they were elected by districts."[15] Whereas districts helped personalize election procedures in the larger states, such tactics were not needed in the smaller ones.

Proponents of the at-large method insisted that the Constitution gave each elector the right to vote for as many candidates as the state had congressmen. "This mode of voting," claimed an author in the *Pennsylvania Mercury*, was "a *federal right* given to them by the Federal Constitution, and which the state *cannot* take from them."[16] By limiting each voter to a choice of one candidate, district elections deprived voters of their full franchise. Some residents of Virginia, noted a congressman, "supposed themselves abridged of nine-tenths of their privilege by being restrained to the choice of one man instead of ten, the number that State sends to this House."[17] According to a New Jersey legislator, election by the people "meant all the inhabitants of the state—that they, by their collected union, should elect the members and not one

---

This State in the Congress of the United States, and for Appointing Electors on the Part of This State for Choosing a President and Vice-President of the United States, and for the Regulation of Said Elections,' and also to Repeal the Act of Assembly Therein Mentioned," December 26, 1791, in *A Digest of the Laws of Maryland* (Baltimore, 1799), 228–30; "South Carolina Election Law," November 4, 1788, in *First Federal Elections*, I: 167–69; "New Hampshire Election Law," November 12, 1788, in *First Federal Elections*, I: 790–92. Because Rhode Island and Delaware had only one congressman each, they had no need to pass an election law. De facto, their elections were at-large.

[14]William Pitt Beers, *An Address to the Legislature and People of the State of Connecticut, on the Subject of Dividing the State into Districts for the Election of Representatives in Congress* (New Haven, Conn., 1791), 33.

[15]Senate, Fourteenth Congress, First Session, March 20, 1816, in *The Debates and Proceedings in the Congress of the United States* (Washington, D.C., 1834), 215 (hereafter cited as *Annals of Congress*).

[16]*Pennsylvania Mercury* (Philadelphia), November 16, 1788, in *First Federal Elections*, I: 274.

[17]House of Representatives, First Congress, First Session, August 22, 1789, in *Annals of Congress*, 801.

part one and another part another."[18] General-ticket elections, advocates maintained, were the most constitutionally sound alternative.

Not surprisingly, supporters of the at-large method at the same time denied the constitutionality of the district system. William Pitt Beers of Connecticut questioned the legal status of election districts, because they were not explicitly provided for in the Constitution. "On what principle," he demanded, "is a new species of political society erected, independent of the majority of the people, unknown to the constitution, and endowed with qualities and powers, which the people of this state have never transferred from themselves?"[19] Others claimed that provisions requiring the candidate to live in his district were unconstitutional additions to the Constitution's established criteria for congressmen.[20] Residency requirements would artificially and needlessly restrict the choice of candidates. "The new Constitution gives me the right to choose as a Pennsylvanian and to elect any Pennsylvanian," proclaimed "A Friend to Agriculture."[21]

The general-ticket system, it was argued, would also guarantee the election of the best qualified men to Congress. Men from throughout the state would come forward and run for office. "The *best men* and the *best abilities*" would be elected.[22] A Pennsylvanian noted in a 1788 letter to Tench Coxe that "by electing out of the state at large you have a better chance of obtaining good men than by obliging the electors to vote for separate Representatives in districts."[23] District elections might force voters to choose among candidates with inferior talents. "The division into districts," asserted a New Yorker in 1788, "supposes what is not true, that genius, abilities, honesty, and other qualifications for legislators, are *equally diffused in a state;* or else debars the freemen the privilege of choosing from among the best qualified."[24] A writer in the *Maryland Journal* dismissed the district system in even harsher terms: "Who are like to be chosen? Is it the man of abilities, who supports a dignity in his character, and independence in his principles, or is it the man who will, probably, have nothing to recommend him but his supposed humility, who will not be too proud to court what are generally called the *poor folks,* shake them by the hand, ask them for their vote

---

[18]*Centinel of Freedom* (Newark, N.J.), March 13, 1789.

[19]Beers, *Address to Connecticut,* 12.

[20]"Pennsylvania Assembly Debates," September 21, 1788, in *First Federal Elections,* I: 283.

[21]"A Friend to Agriculture, Trade and Good Laws to Numa and Pompilius," *Pennsylvania Gazette,* July 30, 1788, in *First Federal Elections,* I: 247.

[22]*Massachusetts Centinel* (Boston), November 1, 1788, in *First Federal Elections,* I: 469.

[23]Thomas Hurley to Tench Coxe, October 6, 1788, in *First Federal Elections,* I: 304.

[24]*Daily Advertiser* (New York), November 7, 1788.

and interest, and, when an opportunity serves, treat them to a can of grog, and whilst drinking of it, join heartily in abusing what are called the *great people?*"[25] District elections promised to supply the nation with a stream of mediocre rulers. Only by drawing on the entire state's pool of talent would the most qualified candidates win election.

Legislators in states with more territory and larger populations, however, came to very different conclusions. The wide variation in attitudes, values, and economic interests within their boundaries would make it difficult for representatives to represent the whole state. The subdivision of states into smaller units meant that each congressman would be more familiar with his constituents' particular interests. Even William Pitt Beers, an advocate of at-large elections, admitted that "some states, from their great extent, or unequal figure, from their being divided by distinct interests, or great natural boundaries, might derive a plausible apology for the institution [of districts]."[26] A New Jersey legislator pointed out that the differentiation between urban and rural interests had something to do with the emergence of the district system. "This method was adopted . . . ," he said, "to counteract . . . the numerous population of those capitals and thus not to swallow up the agricultural by the mercantile interest."[27] The district system gave representation to the full variety of interests contained within a state—a variety more likely to be found in larger states.

Supporters of the district system dismissed the charge that their method was unconstitutional. They insisted that the Constitution gave the states complete freedom in deciding what method to select. "The truth is," wrote "The Moral Politician" of Maryland, "that the Federal Constitution simply enjoins, that Representatives be chosen by the people of the several States, leaving each Legislature at full liberty to direct the *time* which the people should vote, the *place* where they shall vote, and the manner *how* they shall vote."[28] State Representative William Findley of Pennsylvania concurred. He "had never doubted of the powers of the state governments to do what they thought best in this matter," he said.[29] The arguments against district elections, its adherents concluded, were merely obstructionist tactics designed to ensure the election of the majority party's candidates. "Surely it could not be contended," said a New Jersey legislator in 1798, "that persons chosen by districts were not chosen by the people of the states. No man in the state

[25]*Maryland Journal* (Baltimore), November 14, 1788, in *First Federal Elections*, II: 125.

[26]Beers, *Address to Connecticut*, 33.

[27]*State Gazette, and New-Jersey Advertiser* (Trenton), March 13, 1798.

[28]*Maryland Journal*, February 13, 1789, in *First Federal Elections*, II: 219.

[29]"Pennsylvania Assembly Debates," September 24, 1788, in *First Federal Elections*, I: 282.

would lose his privilege to vote by this method—each would vote for one in the several districts, as much in the large as the small, and everyone would be represented."[30] No constitutional impediment existed, according to supporters, to states' choosing the district system.

Adherents of district elections saw their method as a means of mitigating the problems caused by the large size of their states. It helped preserve close contact between people and their representatives. According to "Juniata Man," a congressman representing a whole state was "necessarily a stranger to the greatest part of those who elect him."[31] In districts, however, voters "could enquire of their neighbors" as to a candidate's character and reputation. Citizens were more likely, in the words of the "Real Farmer," to "know, and be known by" their representatives.[32] "The district mode," said one state legislator, "can bring our representatives home to our own doors."[33] It personalized the electoral process, made the ratio between people and representatives more manageable, and lessened the possibility that congressmen would lose touch with their constituents. As the "Real Farmer" put it, districting made federal representation more "equal and *real*."[34]

Supporters of the district system maintained that this method was more likely to ensure responsible representation than were at-large elections. Because both parties would be better acquainted with each other, congressmen would know better what the people wanted—and would be held accountable by their constituents. The impersonality of at-large elections could lead to abuses of power. "Juniata Man" warned that when a representative's election "ceases to depend upon an acquaintance with the persons and character [of those that elect him] . . . , there is little reason to doubt that he will prefer to his public duty, those temptations of personal emolument which his situation offers, and which the price of his vote will always purchase."[35] Under the district plan, a congressman had to answer directly to the small number of people he represented. "The more a representative is under the influence of his constituents," remarked New Jersey legislator William Pennington, "the nearest [they] approach to a free government, and the farther they recede from that, the more they verge toward aristocratical government."[36] Taking a cue from the Antifederalists, advocates of the district system tried to keep the government responsive to the people.

---

[30]*Centinel of Freedom*, March 13, 1798.
[31]*Carlisle Gazette & Western Repository of Knowledge* (Pennsylvania), April 28, 1790.
[32]*Centinel of Freedom*, March 13, 1798; *Hampshire Chronicle* (Massachusetts), October 22, 1788, in *First Federal Elections*, I: 469.
[33]*Centinel of Freedom*, March 28, 1798.
[34]*Hampshire Chronicle*, October 22, 1788, in *First Federal Elections*, I: 469.
[35]*Carlisle Gazette*, April 28, 1790.
[36]*Centinel of Freedom*, March 13, 1798.

Partisan Politics

Exceptions are sometimes useful in demonstrating a general rule. This maxim proves true with regard to the influence of state size in determining the method of electing congressmen. Three states—Pennsylvania, Maryland, and Georgia—did not initially conform to the large state–small state pattern. Another, New Jersey, kept alternating between the electoral methods. After a few years of experimentation, however, all of these states chose the mode most common to states of their size.

Pennsylvania, a large state at the federal Convention and one of the most populous states in the Union, initially had adopted the at-large method of electing congressmen. The Federalists, who dominated the state assembly, instituted the system in an attempt to neutralize Antifederalist sentiment centered in the western part of the state. They hoped that the pro-Constitution majority within the state as a whole would prevent the election of opponents to Congress. Their plan worked. In the first federal elections, Pennsylvanians elected eight Federalist congressmen, most of whom lived in the eastern part of the state.[37]

Almost as soon as the election was over, however, the westerners began a campaign to change the election law. They believed that their region had received little representation in Congress. "Although I have nothing to object to the personal character of our present representatives," said "Juniata Man" in 1790, "I am sure that Pennsylvania will never again suffer eight representatives to be elected out of a mere corner of the state."[38] Regional differentiation within the state caused residents to reject at-large elections. They pressured their legislature to adopt a system that would more adequately reflect the state's diversity. Voting largely by section, the Pennsylvania assembly passed a law in January 1791 dividing the state into eight congressional districts.[39] By

[37]Of the eight, only Frederick Muhlenberg and Thomas Scott were from western areas. See Stanley B. Parsons, William W. Beach, and Dan Hermann, comps., *United States Congressional Districts, 1788–1841* (Westport, Conn., 1978), 20–22; Harry M. Tinkcom, *The Republicans and Federalists in Pennsylvania, 1790–1801* (Harrisburg, Penn., 1950), 25; E. Bruce Thomas, "Political Tendencies in Pennsylvania, 1783–1794" (diss., Temple University, 1938), 157–58; *First Federal Elections*, I: 231–32; "Pennsylvania Election Law," October 4, 1788, in *First Federal Elections*, I: 299–302. In *The Historical Atlas of Political Parties in the United States Congress, 1789–1987* (New York, forthcoming), Kenneth Martis comes to a slightly different conclusion about their party affiliation, claiming that two anti-administration and six pro-administration congressmen were elected. Whatever the slight difference in numbers, my point still holds, however. (See appendix 3.)

[38]*Carlisle Gazette*, April 28, 1790.

[39]*Journal of the First Session of the House of Representatives of the Commonwealth of Pennsylvania* (Philadelphia, 1790), 151–53; Tinkcom, *Republicans and Federalists*, 45–47; "1791 Election Law," in *Acts of Pennsylvania*, 15–17.

switching election procedures, the Pennsylvania legislature acknowledged that a state covering so much territory and encompassing so many
diverse interests needed congressional representatives familiar with each
of its distinctive parts.

In their first congressional elections, Maryland and Georgia experimented with an unusual method of electing congressmen. Although the
states were divided into districts, each elector voted for a representative in
each district. Supporters of this system believed that it combined the best
features of both the district and the at-large methods. "By these means,"
said one advocate, "a knowledge of the local interests of every part of the
state will be carried to Congress, but in such a manner, as not to interfere
with the *general* interest of the whole state."[40] In practice, however, the
system magnified the disadvantages of both methods. As in general-ticket
elections, each person voted for as many candidates as the state had
congressmen. But because the state was divided into districts, the man
elected might not have received a majority of votes in the district he was
to represent. Some Maryland residents protested a system in which
"Washington and Frederick Counties should elect for the People of
Baltimore and Harford Counties, and thereby prevent them from having
the Man of their Choice, and impose on them the Man they very generally
reject—[.]"[41] Furthermore, as in the district system, the plan required
each congressman to live in the district he was to represent, arguably
hindering the election of the best-qualified men in the state.

After these liabilities became apparent in the first elections, legislators
in Maryland and Georgia sought to change their election procedures.
When they did so, delegates in each state chose the option most appropriate for their state's size. Yet by now size was defined more exclusively
in terms of population than territory. According to the 1790 census,
Maryland was one of the larger states, sixth in population among the
original thirteen states. The new election law, passed in December
1791, implemented the district method of electing congressmen.[42]
Georgia, eleventh in population according to the 1790 census, passed a
law in December 1791, requiring at-large elections.[43]

[40]*Pennsylvania Gazette*, July 11, 1788, in *First Federal Elections*, I: 246. See also "Georgia
Election Law," in *First Federal Elections*, II: 256–57; "An Act Directing the Time, Places
and Manner of Holding Elections for Representatives of This State in the Congress of the
United States, and for Appointing Electors on the Part of This State for Choosing a
President and Vice-President of the United States, and for the Regulation of Said Elections," December 22, 1788, in *Laws of Maryland* (Annapolis, n.d.), 337–40.
[41]*Maryland Journal*, February 3, 1789, in *First Federal Elections*, II: 212.
[42]U.S. Bureau of the Census, *The Historical Statistics of the United States* (Washington,
D.C., 1975), I: 24–37; "Maryland's Supplemental Act," December 26, 1791, in *Digest of
Laws of Maryland*, 228–30.
[43]U.S. Bureau of the Census, *Historical Statistics*, I: 24–37; "Georgia's Election Law,"
in *Georgia Session Laws*, 36.

By the mid-1790s most states were keeping the election procedures they had chosen. Although legislators might add new districts, change district boundaries, or tinker with the number of representatives elected by each district, the procedures established by the time of the second congressional elections usually lasted until the federal Apportionment Act of 1842. The one exception was New Jersey. Until 1812, legislators in that state viewed the electoral method as a partisan tool to be used at will to maximize their party's advantage.[44]

Unlike some other states, New Jersey did not at first experience intense controversy over the method of electing congressmen. The New Jersey assembly, dominated by the Federalist West Jersey coalition, passed an at-large election bill in November 1788. As long as the Federalists enjoyed widespread support, the act was unchallenged. The legislature reaffirmed the at-large plan in laws passed in 1790 and 1794.[45]

Discontent, however, grew as the newly formed Republican party began to gain strength in the state. For their own reasons, Republicans began to oppose the at-large method. As early as 1792 a New Brunswick paper commented that there was "some doubt" that the general-ticket system was "altogether agreeable to the wishes of the people."[46] District bills were proposed but voted down in 1792 and 1794.[47] Although the at-large bill passed again in 1794, it succeeded by only a small majority.[48]

By the turn of the century, each party openly regarded the electoral method as a tool of partisan politics, to be used to give the party its maximum number of representatives in Congress. The Federalists, in decline and losing popularity fast, switched positions and began to advocate district elections.[49] No longer able to count on a statewide majority,

---

[44]This is not to say there were no changes in apportionment methods. These changes, however, tended to be infrequent and not undertaken lightly. No other state subjected its election laws to partisan manipulation the way New Jersey did. For a discussion of election methods, see Kenneth C. Martis, *The Historical Atlas of United States Congressional Districts, 1789–1983* (New York, 1982), 4–5.

[45]"An Act to Direct the Time and Mode of Electing Representatives in the Congress of the United States, for This State," November 24, 1790, in *Brunswick Gazette* (New Jersey), November 30, 1790; "An Act Directing the Time and Mode of Electing Representatives in the House of Representatives of the Congress of the United States for This State," November 17, 1794, in *Acts of the Nineteenth General Assembly of the State of New-Jersey* (Trenton, 1795), 928–31; Richard P. McCormick, "New Jersey's First Congressional Election, 1789," *William & Mary Quarterly*, 3d. ser., 6 (1949), 237–50; Richard P. McCormick, *Experiment in Independence: New Jersey in the Critical Period, 1781–1789* (New Brunswick, N.J., 1950), 284, 288–89.

[46]*Brunswick Gazette*, June 12, 1792.

[47]Walter R. Fee, *The Transition from Aristocracy to Democracy in New Jersey, 1789–1829* (Somerville, N.J., 1933), 93.

[48]*Wood's Newark Gazette* (New Jersey), November 12, 1794.

[49]*Centinel of Freedom*, March 13, 1798.

they supported a vastly inequitable districting plan designed to elect as many Federalists as possible. The first district, for example, was to contain approximately 30 percent more people than the third district and over 20 percent more than the second and fourth districts.[50] Although Republicans had long favored district elections, they could not support such a flawed plan. The division, said Mr. Wade, "was too unequal to receive the sanction of any legislature."[51] But solid Federalist support enabled the bill to pass in February 1798.[52]

The Federalists' strategy failed, however. Even with gerrymandered districts, the Federalists succeeded in electing only two Federalist congressmen out of five in 1798.[53] Seeking to rectify their miscalculation, they did another about-face in time for the congressional election of 1800. Just days before the election, they repealed the district bill and reinstated at-large elections.[54] "This was done," said an anonymous Republican critic, "from a confidence of their own strength being adequate to secure the whole representation."[55] Once again, however, the maneuver failed. All five of New Jersey's congressional seats went to Republicans.[56]

The next year New Jerseyites elected a Republican governor and a predominantly Republican legislature.[57] Now that the Republicans were the majority party, they were able to pass whatever election laws they pleased. At-large election laws were approved in 1803, 1806, and 1807.[58] Seeking to preserve their residual support in the state, the Federalists urged the adoption of a district law. The Republicans, however, would have no part of it. Citing the Federalists' previous attempts to manipulate the system to their own advantage, one New Jersey Re-

[50]Parsons, Beach, and Hermann, *Congressional Districts*, 50; *Centinel of Freedom*, March 13 1798 and March 28, 1798.

[51]*Centinel of Freedom*, March 13, 1798.

[52]*Votes and Proceedings of the Twenty-Second General Assembly of the State of New-Jersey* (Trenton, 1798), 44–46; "An Act Directing the Time and Mode of Electing Representatives in the House of Representatives of the Congress of the United States," March 1, 1798, in *Acts of the Twenty-Second General Assembly of the State of New Jersey* (Trenton, 1798), 310–12.

[53]Parsons, Beach, and Hermann, *Congressional Districts*, 50.

[54]"An Act Directing the Time and Mode of Electing Representatives in the House of Representatives of the Congress of the United States, for This State," November 7, 1800, in *Acts of the Twenty-Fifth General Assembly of the State of New Jersey* (Trenton, 1800), 4–6; Harold F. Wilson, *Outline History of New Jersey* (New Brunswick, N.J., 1950), 92; *Centinel of Freedom*, November 24, 1812.

[55]*Carolina Gazette* (Charleston), December 23, 1802.

[56]Parsons, Beach, and Hermann, *Congressional Districts*, 50.

[57]Wilson, *Outline of New Jersey History*, 92.

[58]"An Act Directing the Time and Mode of Electing Electors of the President and Vice-President of the United States, and Representatives in Congress, on the Part of This State," December 3, 1807, in *Laws of the State of New-Jersey* (Trenton, 1811), 39–45; *Centinel of Freedom*, October 18, 1803 and November 24, 1807.

publican asserted in 1802: "It is impossible to enumerate the absurdities which have marked the career of the federalists of this state. Devoid of every other motive, but as will gratify their ambition or avarice, their professions of patriotism are always refuted by the selfish means they employ to effect their real designs."[59] Now that the Republicans had control, they would use the system most advantageous to their party.

The Republicans, however, received a rude shock in the election of 1812. The Federalists played on popular opposition to the war against Great Britain—a war that the Republicans wanted to fight—and succeeded in regaining control of New Jersey's lower house in that year.[60] Once in office, they immediately moved to consolidate their gains in time for the federal elections. On November 7, 1812, the legislature passed a bill dividing the state into three congressional districts, each of which would elect two congressmen.[61] This measure, the Federalists believed, would ensure the election of at least four Federalist congressmen.[62] Outraged Republicans claimed that the Federalists had acted "with a versatility that betrays the weakness of their cause," passing a law that was a "deadly poisoned arrow, levelled with certain aim at the inestimable right of suffrage."[63]

The Federalist triumph, however, was short-lived. The party had overestimated its popularity yet again and succeeded in electing only three Federalists of six.[64] The following September, the Federalists lost control of the state legislature.[65] Moving just as quickly as their opponents had, the Republicans worked to change the election law once they were back in office. On November 2, 1813, the legislature voted to repeal the previous law and reinstate an 1807 law that revived general-ticket elections.[66] From that time until the Apportionment Act of 1842 (with a brief exception in the 1828 elections), New Jersey continued to use the at-large method of electing congressmen.[67] At long last the state had settled on a single procedure and had taken the issue out of the realm of partisan politics.

What is significant about this comic tale is less New Jersey's manip-

[59]*Carolina Gazette*, December 23, 1802.
[60]Wilson, *Outline of New Jersey History*, 93–94; *Centinel of Freedom*, October 20, 1812.
[61]"An Act Directing the Time and Mode of Electing Representatives in Congress on the Part of This State," November 7, 1812, in *Acts of the Thirty-Seventh General Assembly of the State of New Jersey* (Trenton, 1812), 5–11.
[62]*Centinel of Freedom*, November 3, 1812.
[63]Ibid., November 24, 1812 and November 31, 1812.
[64]Parsons, Beach, and Hermann, *Congressional Districts*, 170–72.
[65]Wilson, *Outline of New Jersey History*, 95.
[66]"An Act to Repeal the act . . . of 1812; and to Revive the Act . . . of 1807," November 3, 1813, in *Acts of the Thirty-Eighth General Assembly of the State of New Jersey* (Trenton, 1814), 60–61; *Centinel of Freedom*, October 19, 1813 and November 16, 1813.
[67]Martis, *Atlas of Congressional Districts*, 4.

ulation of the law for partisan purposes than the absence of such machi-
nations in the other states. The New Jersey example vividly demon-
strates how easily election laws could become a partisan tool. Yet even
New Jersey legislators finally realized that the election laws should not
be handled so cavalierly. It was no coincidence, however, that the state
settled on at-large elections. After having experienced both methods,
the legislators realized that the general-ticket system was more appropriate for New Jersey's limited population and small territory.

Despite the growth of the two-party system,[68] other state legislatures
exercised more restraint. Most states kept the same basic method from
the time of the second congressional election until the Apportionment
Act of 1842, when all the states were forced to conform to the district
plan.[69] Having found the most suitable method for their state's size,
legislators preferred to keep their hands off the federal elections. By
1812, then, the division between large and small states in the method of
electing congressmen was complete. (See appendix 3.)

The First Gerrymander

A state's method of electing its congressmen reflected larger assumptions about representation—about whom and what the legislator represented in Congress. The small states' adoption of the at-large method
was consistent with the states' continuing adherence to spatial assumptions about representation. The state remained, in their thinking, an
indivisible unit of representation. "So it is," said one commentator,
"that the people at large choose for the state at large, and the persons so
chosen represents [*sic*] the whole state."[70] The states as territorial communities deserved representation. If the framers had wanted Americans
to be represented strictly according to population, said William Pitt
Beers, they could have abolished existing state boundaries and "made a
new division of territory, without regarding pre-established boundaries,
and accommodated to all a uniform election law."[71] Since they did not
do so, congressmen, he concluded, "may properly be said to represent
the state as a community."[72]

[68]Richard Hofstadter, *The Idea of a Party System: The Rise of Legitimate Opposition in the United States, 1780–1840* (Berkeley, Calif., 1969), 40–73.

[69]Richard Peters, comp., *The Public Statutes at Large of the United States of America* (Boston, 1846), 491, chap. 47.

[70]"Pennsylvania Assembly Debates," September 24, 1788, in *First Federal Elections*, I: 284.

[71]Beers, *Address to Connecticut*, 11.

[72]Ibid., 10.

Supporters of at-large elections argued that districting would cause congressmen to be confused about where their primary allegiance lay: with the district or with the state. Representatives, they feared, would place the interests of their districts over those of the state. In order to get reelected, they would seek to please a narrow constituency at the expense of the larger public good.[73] Whereas the general-ticket system "united the members for a state more together in one interest,"[74] the district system split representatives into individuals representing separate, even competing, interests. "Will [those elected by districts] feel themselves responsible to the whole state?" asked New Jersey legislator Stewart. "No," he replied, "only to the party in the district who sent them."[75] Beers of Connecticut warned, "Divide the state into districts, remove the responsibility from your representatives, and the districts, like atoms repelled from their proper vortex, will feel new attractions, fly to other centers, associate and adhere to other bodies."[76] Only general-ticket elections could guarantee that the states' interests would be represented in the lower house of Congress.

Small-state legislators thus continued to believe that the states should be represented as states—not just in the Senate, where each state received an equal vote, but also in the House of Representatives. General-ticket elections provided them with the means of perpetuating this view. They ignored the Federalist view, which was to eliminate the kind of localism and state particularism that had been so damaging to the Confederation.[77] During the debate in New York over the proper method of electing congressmen, an opponent of at-large elections warned, "The general government has nothing to fear from district prejudice, but from the more *enlarged prejudice* towards individual states"[78]—a prejudice presumably encouraged by the general-ticket system. Small-state representatives rejected this warning.

Legislators in the large states, by contrast, had chosen the district system because it would better reflect the diversity within their borders. They considered the state as an amalgam of many different—even conflicting—interests. They recognized, however, that congressmen repre-

---

[73]As one critic put it, a congressman would become consumed with the desire to "pleas[e] a few of his neighbors by bringing a post road near their plantations" and with other such trivial, local concerns. *Pennsylvania Mercury*, September 16, 1788, in *First Federal Elections*, I: 274.

[74]*Centinel of Freedom*, March 13, 1798.

[75]Ibid., March 28, 1798.

[76]Beers, *Address to Connecticut*, 28.

[77]Gordon S. Wood, *The Creation of the American Republic, 1776–1787* (New York, 1969), 463–67, 506–18.

[78]*Daily Advertiser*, November 10, 1788.

sented the national interest rather than the particular interests of the people who elected them. Whereas a congressman elected by general ticket was supposed to promote his home state's interests, the district-elected congressman was free to serve the broader national community. New Jersey state legislator Pennington commented that among congressmen elected by districts, "there might be a difference of opinion in trivial matters, but when the general interest was concerned, [I have] no doubt but they would unite to a man."[79] District elections were thus more likely than at-large elections to produce the kind of public servant that Federalists had envisioned.

Also, in contrast to the small states, the large states thought about representation in demographic terms. The decision to elect by district forced state legislators to make numerous subsequent decisions that those in general-ticket states did not face. They had to decide how to divide their states and on what basis district lines should be drawn. In adopting district elections, residents of the large states affirmed and expanded their acceptance of population-based representative institutions.

Once legislators had decided to divide their state into districts, they had to determine what constituted a district. They knew that individual towns, counties, and parishes were not populous enough to warrant representation in Congress. Although the legislators took care not to dismember existing political units,[80] in most states they had to create new units for congressional elections—"a new species of political society," as Beers put it.[81] Most states were split into as many districts as they had congressmen—a method called the single-district system. A small number of states also included a few plural districts, which gave very populous areas two or three congressmen; but this method disappeared rather quickly.[82]

State legislators realized that for representation to be kept equitable, each district should contain approximately the same number of people. As the population changed, however, district lines would have to be periodically redrawn. A New York assemblyman objected to this procedure, arguing, "The continual increase of the state would render it

[79]*Centinel of Freedom*, March 13, 1798.

[80]*New-Hampshire Spy* (Portsmouth), November 10, 1788; *State Gazette, & New Jersey Advertiser* (Trenton), March 13, 1798. See also the wording of election laws cited in this chapter.

[81]Beers, *Address to Connecticut*, 12.

[82]John L. Moore, ed., *Congressional Quarterly's Guide to U.S. Elections* (Washington, D.C., 1985), 690; Martis, *Atlas of Congressional Districts*, 4–5.

necessary to pass a new bill every year or two; our election law therefore, could only be a temporary one."[83]

Despite the inconvenience, legislators regarded population equality among congressional districts as crucial. In the first federal elections, legislators did not yet have the results of the federal census. As a result, the districts that were created varied widely in size. The largest districts in Massachusetts, New York, and South Carolina, for example, had twice as many people as the smallest districts in those states.[84] Districts in the other states fell in the whole range between these extremes. After 1792, however, when federal census data became available, legislators began to equalize the populations of congressional districts. Although some large disparities still existed, from 1788 to 1812 the number of people in each state's districts became progressively more equal.[85] By 1813, some New Jersey state legislators scorned an inequitable districting plan, contending that, "By dividing the state into partial and unequal districts, [the plan] destroys the most important principle of republican government, that representation should bear a due proportion to population."[86]

Yet, even with population as a guide to creating districts, state legislators still lacked a rule that would help them determine where within the state to draw district lines. "As the general interests of a state have little or no relation to geographical divisions, the districts must be formed upon false or fanciful principles," concluded Beers of Connecticut, an opponent of districting.[87] Supporters of the district system, however, realized that their own political sentiments provided an organizing principle. The political party or faction that controlled the state assembly could group counties and towns into congressional districts in such a way as to promote the fortunes of their candidates. Even in the early years of the republic, when party lines were fluid and not well-defined, politicians could see the potential for party affiliation as the basis for districting.

[83]*Daily Advertiser*, December 19, 1788.

[84]In the first federal elections, Massachusetts' districts ranged in population size from 39,594 to 89,972; New York's from 38,845 to 103,850; and South Carolina's from 26,284 to 69,301. These states obviously represent extreme cases, but other states also had substantial disparities among their districts. These figures are based on my calculation of the represented populations in each district (all whites plus three-fifths of all blacks). Raw numbers are found in Parsons, Beach, and Hermann, *Congressional Districts*, 10, 16–18, 26.

[85]Parsons, Beach, and Hermann, *Congressional Districts*, 2–143. For statistical proof of this trend, see Rosemarie Zagarri, "The Emergence of the Extensive Republic: Representation in the United States, 1776 to 1812" (diss., Yale University, 1984), app. 6.

[86]"An Act to Repeal the Act . . . of 1812; and to Revive the Act . . . of 1807," November 3, 1813, in *Acts of the Thirty-Eighth General Assembly of the State of New Jersey*, 19.

[87]Beers, *Address to Connecticut*, 30.

The districting process in Virginia in 1788 provides a good example of how political leaders grasped the art of drawing districts well before the term *gerrymandering* was coined in 1812. The Antifederalists held a slight majority in the Virginia legislature. When the assembly began to divide the state into districts, they tried to draw the district boundaries in such a way as to maximize Antifederalist strength in the state and elect as many Antifederalist congressmen as possible. Their more specific goal was to defeat arch-Federalist James Madison in his race against Antifederalist James Monroe.

The Antifederalists had blocked Madison's election to the Senate. When Madison claimed to prefer a seat in the House of Representatives, the Antifederalists did everything in their power to prevent his election there too. As they organized the state into congressional districts, they made sure that Madison's home county, Orange, was lumped into an otherwise predominantly Antifederalist region.[88]

Madison's supporters immediately realized what was happening. A correspondent to the *Virginia Independent Chronicle* claimed that the Antifederalists had "distorted" Madison's district into "a thousand excentrick angles" in order to ensure his defeat.[89] The spectacle outraged many residents. "The prevalence of local prejudices," wrote a fellow Virginian to Madison, "are not uncommon in our house—but for a majority to bend its utmost efforts ag[ains]t an individual is rather uncommon—The object of the majority to day has been to prevent *yr.* Election in the house of Representatives."[90] In a letter to Madison, Burgess Ball concluded, "The Counties annexed to yours are arranged so, as to render your Election, I fear, extremely doubtful, the greater no. being Antifederal."[91] To everyone's surprise, Madison beat Monroe by 336 votes.[92] Yet, although the Antifederalists were unsuccessful in Madison's case, they did succeed in electing four Antifederalist congressmen of ten.[93]

Gerrymandering, then, is as old as the district system and a direct

[88]Richard R. Beeman, *The Old Dominion and the New Nation, 1788–1801* (Charlottesville, Va., 1971), 19.

[89]*Virginia Independent Chronicle* (Richmond), March 11, 1789, in *First Federal Elections*, II: 393n.i.

[90]George Lee Turberville to James Madison, November 13, 1788, in *First Federal Elections*, II: 372.

[91]Burgess Ball to James Madison, December 8, 1788, in *First Federal Elections*, II: 323. See also II: 310–45.

[92]*Virginia Herald* (Fredericksburg), February 12, 1789, in *First Federal Elections*, II: 346.

[93]Kenneth R. Bowling, "Politics in the First Congress, 1789–1791" (diss., University of Wisconsin, 1968), 345–47. In his *Historical Atlas of Political Parties*, Martis comes to a slightly different conclusion, claiming that there were three anti-administration congressmen and seven pro-administration congressmen. (See appendix 3.)

consequence of its use.[94] From the beginning, state legislators recognized the power of districting as a partisan tool—and were not reluctant to use it. States that elected by general ticket had no opportunity to develop mechanisms such as gerrymandering in their federal elections. Because every elector voted for as many candidates as the state had congressmen, there were no smaller-sized constituencies within these states. As a result, congressional elections came to be less politicized in the small states than in the large.

Districts and Diversity

As in their choice of state capitals, methods of apportionment in the state legislatures, and systems of representation for Congress, legislators from the large and the small states differed in their choice of the proper procedure for electing federal representatives. Continuing to think spatially about representation questions, citizens in smaller states believed that the state as a territorial community should be represented in the lower house of Congress. Because each person would vote for as many candidates as the state had congressmen, the individual congressman was to represent the interests of the entire state in the national legislature. In the larger states, however, legislators thought about representation in demographic terms. They regarded the state as an amalgam of diverse interests that an accident of history had united into a single unit. They understood equitable representation to mean that equal numbers of people within the state would receive an equal number of representatives, and they drew their district boundary lines accordingly. Population rather than territory defined their notion of representation.

The difference in electoral procedures between large and small states produced a difference in the function of political parties. In large, districted states, politicians actively tried to advance their party's interests through the drawing of district boundaries. They gerrymandered districts to get their candidates elected. Small states electing by general

[94]According to the *Oxford English Dictionary*, *gerrymander* is "a method of arranging election districts so that the political party making the arrangement will be enabled to elect a greater number of representatives than they could on a fair system and more than they should in proportion to their numerical strength." The term apparently originated in Massachusetts in 1812, when the Democrat-controlled state legislature drew district boundaries so contorted that they formed the image of a salamander. Elbridge Gerry was governor at the time, and his name was combined with the last two syllables of *salamander* to describe what the legislature had wrought. *The Compact Edition of the Oxford English Dictionary*, s.v. "gerrymander." See also Moore, *Congressional Quarterly's Guide to U.S. Elections*, 691.

ticket, however, had no such vehicle to promote their party's interests. The majority party in the state would send almost all the delegates to Congress. But politicians from the districted states may have succeeded too well. This difference in electoral methods produced a difference in the partisan character of the states' congressional delegations. Whereas congressmen elected by general ticket tended to belong to a single party, those elected by districts tended to be from more than one party. (See appendix 3.) This simple fact would soon come to hold ominous implications for the future of large- and small-state relations in Congress.

CHAPTER 6

The Persistence of the
Large State–Small State Conflict

Contrary to accepted interpretations, the conflict between large and small states did not end at the Constitutional Convention. It resurfaced in several forms for more than a half-century following the Convention. To be sure, the division based on size emerged only in a particular context—during congressional disputes over representation issues—and never extended to the general population. Despite its limited scope, the persistence of the conflict had significant implications for sectional politics during the antebellum era.

From 1789 to 1850, three issues consistently mobilized the alliances based on state size: the dispute over whether congressmen should be elected by districts or at large, a related debate over whether presidential electors should be elected by districts or at large, and finally, the decennial conflict over reapportionment of the House of Representatives. Although the exact composition of the coalitions changed over time, one group of states continued to identify itself as small and the other as large. Both sides, moreover, continued to assume that a state's size provided the key to its potential population, with states having less territory sustaining fewer people and those with more land sustaining more people. In the end, the basis for the division had to be legislated out of existence.

All the Salvation We Have

Within a decade after the first federal elections, the difference among states in their method of electing congressmen had become a subject of contention in Congress itself. Each state had decided independently of the others on the procedure it would follow, but by the second congressional elections the pattern was clear: small states were using the at-large method, and large states were using the district system. (See appendix 4.) As the two-party system solidified, this distinction came to have a heightened significance.

As Americans soon discovered, the manner of election influenced the partisan composition of a state's congressional delegation. Under the general-ticket system, each person voted for as many candidates as the state had congressmen. If a majority of people favored one party over the other, the congressmen would all be members of the same political party. The district system, however, gave a voice to smaller constituencies within the state. Since each district elected its own congressman, local support for a minority-party candidate could translate into that candidate's election to Congress. Whereas the minority would be overwhelmed by the majority in an at-large election, the minority gained spokesmen through the districting procedure. This difference resulted in more politically unified congressional delegations for states electing by general ticket and more divided delegations for states electing by district.

The convolutions in New Jersey were a case in point. In 1796, the state's general-ticket congressional election had sent five Federalists to the House of Representatives. Two years later, the switch to the district system resulted in the election of three Republicans and two Federalists.[1] These two elections demonstrated how general-ticket elections masked local sentiments for minority candidates. Had the 1796 election been by district, it probably would have reflected the beginnings of the Republican surge. Whereas the minority's voice was lost in at-large elections, it gained expression in 1798 through the district system. The difference in electoral method alone produced a marked alteration in the composition of New Jersey's congressional delegation.

As a direct result of the electoral procedure used, small states sent more politically unified delegations to Congress than did large states. A small state voting by general ticket usually elected congressmen belonging to the same political party, whereas a large state electing by district sent members from two or more parties. A sample of every fifth Congress from 1789 to 1839 confirms the persistence of this pattern throughout the entire period. (See appendix 3.) With few exceptions, the large-state congressional delegations tended to be more politically divided than those from the small states.

[1]Stanley B. Parsons, William W. Beach, and Dan Hermann, comps., *United States Congressional Districts, 1788–1841* (Westport, Conn., 1978), 48, 50.

Common party affiliation meant that the members of a delegation were more likely to vote together. Although small-state representatives from different states might not be from the same party, they would all share the small-state point of view. If a particular issue affected their interests, they could more easily band together than their large-state neighbors to vote as a bloc. When they did vote as a bloc, they exercised an influence disproportionate to their numbers in the lower house.

Both large- and small-state delegates acknowledged the implications of the system. The small states admitted that they deliberately used the at-large system to gain greater power than they deserved in the lower house. Arguing against the use of the district method in his state in 1798, a New Jersey legislator commented that district elections "tend to dis-unite [the representatives'] sentiments, which would operate to great injury. All the salvation we have . . . is to have our few members united. A different mode might be useful in extensive and populous states, but that can be no guide for us."[2] Many congressmen from larger states resented what they saw as a violation of the constitutional compact, which gave the large states unquestioned superiority in the House of Representatives. According to Congressman Edward Everett of Massachusetts, "The general ticket system was adopted by some of the smaller States, because it gave them political power over the larger."[3] Congressman John Campbell of South Carolina pointed out in 1842, "Georgia, New Jersey, and Alabama now elect by general ticket; and the consequence was, that, though they were entitled to comparatively small numbers of Representatives, yet, on all party questions, they had a stronger voice than the largest States, who went on the district plan."[4] By using the general-ticket system, the small states had mounted a challenge to the large states' dominance in the lower house.

Some, however, doubted that a small-state voting bloc had much influence. Congressman Samuel Mitchill of New York, for example, pointed out that the small-state threat was minimal precisely because representatives voted as individuals, not as states. He remarked in 1810 "that gentlemen did not vote by States, but *per capita*. How often," he asked, "did gentlemen coming from the same State, vote as differently as if they came from the most remote part of the Union. The fact was, that members of the House voted by polls, each according to what his

[2]*State Gazette, & New-Jersey Advertiser* (Trenton), March 13, 1798.

[3]House of Representatives, Twenty-Seventh Congress, Second Session, May 2, 1842, in *Congressional Globe*, 11 (May 2, 1842), 464. See also Joel Francis Paschal, "The House of Representatives: 'Grand Depository of the Democratic Principle,'" *Law and Contemporary Problems*, 17 (Spring 1952), 281.

[4]House of Representatives, Twenty-Seventh Congress, Second Session, April 26, 1842, in *Congressional Globe*, 11 (April 28, 1842), 445.

sense of duty dictate. Therefore," he said, "there was no ground for this question about influence of States, as such, in the House."[5] Mitchill was correct in claiming that the states did not form coalitions based on state size when voting on most substantive issues, including volatile topics such as slavery, tariffs, and taxation. Yet when Congress debated procedural questions concerning representation, such as apportionment, districting, and the ratio of people to representatives, large and small states' differences did come into play.

By 1800, large-state representatives in Congress had decided that at-large elections should be eliminated. Districting, they believed, should be imposed uniformly throughout the country. The district system, they said, was more fair and equitable. In the same year, Congressman John Nicholas of Virginia introduced a constitutional amendment that would require the use of the district system in the election of both congressmen and presidential electors. After deliberating for two months, a House committee rejected the proposal.[6]

The issue, however, kept cropping up. Throughout the early years of the century, various state legislatures sent petitions to Congress urging that general-ticket elections be abolished. The large states attempted to quash the challenge to their power.[7] North Carolina's governor declared in 1812 "that the large states ought in justice and policy to counteract this undue weight of the small states."[8] Intermittently but repeatedly from 1800 through 1842, Congress entertained laws and constitutional amendments designed to abolish the general-ticket method of electing representatives. At least thirty-four resolutions on this matter were introduced between 1800 and 1826 alone.[9]

For a variety of reasons, the measures failed. Many congressmen believed that the Constitution gave the states unambiguous authority over establishing the manner of electing their federal representatives. Congress could intervene, they thought, only in cases where states had

[5]House of Representatives, Eleventh Congress, Third Session, December 17, 1810, in *The Debates and Proceedings in the Congress of the United States* (Washington, D.C., 1834), 428 (hereafter cited as *Annals of Congress*).

[6]House of Representatives, Sixth Congress, Second Session, in *Annals of Congress*, November 21, 1800, 785; January 22, 1801, 941–60.

[7]S. Dana Horton, *Proportional Representation* (Philadelphia, 1873), 14–15; John L. Moore, ed., *Congressional Quarterly's Guide to U.S. Elections* (Washington, D.C., 1985), 690.

[8]*Star* (Raleigh, N.C.), December 4, 1812.

[9]*Annals of Congress:* Eighth Congress, First Session, 95–105, 663–67; Twelfth Congress, Second Session, 57–58, 848–49; Thirteenth Congress, Second Session, 797–98; Fourteenth Congress, First Session, 158; Fourteenth Congress, Second Session, 256–57; Seventeenth Congress, First Session, 551–52; Eighteenth Congress, First Session, 43–46, 801, 850–66; Herman V. Ames, *The Proposed Amendments to the Constitution of the United States during the First Century of Its History* (New York, 1970; orig. publ. 1896), 56–59.

grossly abused their power. Others simply deferred to the state legislators' greater understanding of their states' needs and circumstances.[10]
Finally, a built-in opposition to changes in the election law existed in
Congress. Between 1789 and 1842, as much as 31 percent of the total
House membership came from states that elected their congressmen by
general ticket and that opposed any alteration in the status quo.[11] Even
more importantly, the Senate, where the small states had their greatest
strength, exercised effective veto power over any proposals to eliminate
at-large elections.

The showdown came in 1842. After receiving the results of the 1840
census, Congress took up its decennial task of reapportioning seats in
the lower house. During the debate, Whig representatives introduced an
amendment to the apportionment bill that required district elections for
congressmen. This amendment unleashed a bitter controversy that split
Whigs and Democrats, northerners and southerners, and, perhaps most
important of all, large and small states. But by then the power of the
small-state coalition had been diminished. Only ten of the twenty-six
states in the Union used at-large elections.[12] Small states were thus
outnumbered in the Senate as well as in the House. No large states
seemed interested in rescuing them, either.

Both sides rehashed arguments that had by this time become thor-
oughly familiar. Small-state supporters of the at-large method emphasized each state's constitutional right to choose its own method of electing congressmen. Federal representatives, they said, represented the
state as a community. All the people in a state, then, should be able to
vote for all of the state's congressmen. Districting would only promote a
dangerous particularism. Senator Arthur Bagby of Alabama, for instance,
said that "it would be wholly out of place to introduce local influences
into a National Legislature, intended to represent the people of a State
collectively, in reference to matters of national import, or affecting the
interests of States."[13] Conversely, large-state adherents of the district
system insisted that Congress did have a right to direct the manner of

[10]*Speech of Mr. Charles Atherton of New Hampshire, in Committee of the Whole on the State of the
Union, on the Apportionment Bill* (Washington, D.C., May 3, 1842), 1–9.

[11]Kenneth C. Martis, *The Historical Atlas of United States Congressional Districts, 1789–
1983* (New York, 1982), 4. Martis's figures do not take into account the states that had only
one vote and hence, in effect, voted at large. If this figure were included, the percentage
of general-ticket states would be even higher.

[12]Martis, *Atlas of Congressional Districts*, 4. They were Alabama, Arkansas, Delaware,
Georgia, Michigan, Mississippi, Missouri, New Hampshire, New Jersey, and Rhode
Island.

[13]Senate, Twenty-Seventh Congress, Second Session, June 3, 1842, in *Congressional
Globe*, 11 (June 6, 1842), 572.

election and that, in the interest of fairness, the method should be uniform nationwide. Furthermore, they maintained that district elections guaranteed a closer relationship between representatives and constituents than the general-ticket system did. "In order to have a correct representation," said Senator William Graham of North Carolina, "there should be something of intimacy between the Representative and his constituents, so that he might explain to them the opinions which he entertained of public affairs, and give to them an account of his stewardship. This was the case where the district system was in force, but not so with the general-ticket system."[14]

What differentiated the 1842 conflict from previous debates was that several small states that still elected by general ticket came to support the districting measure. It was an incident in Alabama that had prompted the bill's introduction. In 1840, Democrats in the Alabama state legislature had switched the state from district to at-large elections in an effort to get more members of their party elected to Congress.[15] Whigs in Congress, who believed the district system benefited their party, were outraged.

The Whigs argued that the Alabama action was just the beginning of a more general movement toward at-large elections. Just as states had eventually adopted general-ticket elections for presidential electors, so would they soon all turn toward at-large elections of congressmen. As the Whigs told it, such a move would be disastrous for the small states. If all states had at-large elections, the large-state delegations could be as internally unified as the small. The large states, however, had many more representatives than the small states did. Not only would the small states lose whatever extra influence at-large elections had given them in the lower house, but they would become a completely inconsequential force there. Edward Everett of Massachusetts warned, "The idea [of a general ticket] . . . had been broached [by the large states], and it was possible it might ere long be adopted; and if it was, the smaller States must be swallowed up; in which case, the Union could not be expected long to endure."[16] Representative John Campbell of South Carolina made a similar prediction: "The large States . . . would soon resort to the plan of a general ticket; and then what became of the influence of the small States? They must be lost, and swallowed up."[17] If each state

[14]Ibid., 573.

[15]Ibid., 567; Johanna Nicol Shields, "Whigs Reform the 'Bear Garden': Representation and the Apportionment Act of 1842," *Journal of the Early Republic*, 5 (Fall 1985), 362–63. The law became effective in the 1842 election and was repealed afterwards.

[16]House of Representatives, Twenty-Seventh Congress, Second Session, May 2, 1842, in *Congressional Globe*, 11 (May 2, 1842), 464.

[17]House of Representatives, Twenty-Seventh Congress, Second Session, April 26, 1842, in *Congressional Globe*, 11 (April 28, 1842), 445.

could cast its vote as a single bloc—a capability that at-large elections would give them—then the small states' votes, both individually and collectively, would dwindle into complete insignificance.

The Whigs' districting bill fractured the small-state coalition. In a complete reversal of their former position, some small states began to support the nationwide districting law. Districting, they thought, would prevent an even worse possibility—the universal adoption of at-large elections. In the end, the support of senators and representatives from small states such as New Hampshire, Georgia, Missouri, and Mississippi, which still had general-ticket elections, was crucial to the passage of the bill.[18] The provision requiring district elections for congressmen in every state was attached to the 1842 Reapportionment Act. It stipulated, "In every case where a State is entitled to more than one Representative, the number to which each State shall be entitled . . . shall be elected by districts compiled of contiguous territory equal in number to the number of Representatives to which said State may be entitled, no one district electing more than one Representative."[19] The alliance of Whigs and of certain small-state representatives helped achieve victory for a plan that large-state delegates had long supported.

Although the 1842 act expired within ten years, the principle of district elections had been firmly established. The legal tradition for the method had won approval. Districting laws were passed in 1862, 1872, and throughout the early years of the twentieth century. Subsequent Supreme Court decisions in the mid-twentieth century reaffirmed the principle.[20] With the demise of general-ticket elections, an important manifestation of the division between large and small states had been forcibly eliminated.

Choosing Presidential Electors

At the same time that large and small states were debating the districting question, the split reappeared in another area, this time over the proper method of choosing presidential electors. As it had with congressmen, the Constitution gave each state legislature the right to determine its own method of selecting presidential electors. Electors could be

---

[18]House of Representatives, Twenty-Seventh Congress, Second Session, May 3, 1842, in *Congressional Globe*, 11 (May 10, 1842), 471; Senate, Twenty-Seventh Congress, Second Session, June 8, 1842, in *Congressional Globe*, 11 (June 11, 1842), 597.

[19]Richard Peters, comp., *The Public Statutes At Large of the United States of America* (Boston, 1846), 491, chap. 47; Emanuel Celler, "Congressional Apportionment—Past, Present, and Future," *Law and Contemporary Problems*, 17 (Spring 1952), 272.

[20]Moore, *Congressional Quarterly's Guide to U.S. Elections*, 690–92.

chosen by the legislature or elected by the people. In 1789, for example, only four states held direct popular elections for electors; the rest allowed their state legislatures to choose.[21] Over time, however, as more states began to allow the people to vote in the presidential elections, state legislators confronted the question of whether electors should be elected by districts or at large. Although the problem was similar to that faced by states in congressional elections, legislators had to create different districts for the election of presidential electors, because each state had two more electors than it had congressmen.[22]

By 1800 Congress had become aware of a growing distinction between states that used the district system and those that elected by general ticket—a distinction based on state size. As the congressmen saw it, the large states tended to vote for their electors by districts and the small states selected them at large—just as they did in congressional elections. This difference gave the small states a power in presidential elections disproportionate to their populations. Whereas the general-ticket system gave all of a state's electoral votes to the candidate with the most votes in that state, the district system divided the state's electoral votes among more than one candidate. As a senator from North Carolina explained it in 1816, "A small state, unanimous for one candidate, might by general ticket counterbalance the weight of two large States voting by districts."[23] A minority of states could potentially control a majority of the presidential electors, a situation that undermined the notion of majority rule. Senator James Barbour of Virginia observed, "In consequence of the elections by districts in the large States and by general ticket in the small States, an undue preponderance had been given . . . to the small States in the councils of the nation."[24] The large states believed that the small states were manipulating election procedures in order to heighten their own influence and diminish that of the large states.

As early as 1800, some congressmen began advocating the passage of a law or a constitutional amendment requiring the district election of presidential electors. Throughout the early years of the nineteenth century, such proposals were submitted and resubmitted, at least thirty of them between 1800 and 1826. Supporters argued that the general-ticket system silenced the minority's voice and prevented an adequate representation of all views within the state. Small-state representatives, however,

---

[21]Ibid., 254–55.

[22]See *Pennsylvania Packet* (Philadelphia), September 27, 1788, in *The Documentary History of the First Federal Elections, 1788–1790*, ed. Merrill Jensen and Robert A. Becker (Madison, Wis., 1976), I: 290–91.

[23]Senate, Fourteenth Congress, First Session, March 20, 1816, in *Annals of Congress*, 219.

[24]Senate, Fourteenth Congress, First Session, May 20, 1816, in *Annals of Congress*, 214.

insisted that the Constitution gave them complete authority over the method of selecting presidential electors and that Congress could intervene only if the states severely misused their power. Despite the large states' strong feelings on the matter, the districting measures consistently failed to receive enough votes to become law.[25]

In time, it became clear that the large states had found another solution to the problem. By 1820 more and more states were switching to the general-ticket system and abandoning the district method. Even the large states began to choose their presidential electors in this fashion.[26] Large-state representatives argued that they had opted for this procedure out of "self-defence." Senator Barbour said in 1816:

> Under the district system, Pennsylvania exhibited a melancholy spectacle; whilst the small Eastern States gave many votes, the weight of Pennsylvania, great as she is, dwindled down to a solitary vote. . . . To regain her station in the Union, she was compelled to follow the example. Virginia, also, obliged by inevitable necessity, arising from the principle of self-preservation requiring her to counterpoise that system which had made its appearance in another quarter of the Union, reluctantly resorted to [the general ticket system].[27]

In effect, the small states' use of at-large elections compelled the large states to switch to the method.

By 1836, popular elections for presidential electors by general ticket had become universal, except in South Carolina, which continued to have its legislature vote for president.[28] In a sense, the small states' method had triumphed. In the process, however, the small states had lost the advantage that the at-large system had given them. Because both the large and the small states now used the same method, each state's electoral votes would most likely go to a single individual. Because the large states had more people, they had many more votes than the smaller ones. The small states' disproportionate influence on presidential elections, then, had effectively been eliminated. The large states had beat them at their own game.

---

[25]For example, see *Annals of Congress:* Sixth Congress, Second Session, 785, 941–46; Eighth Congress, First Session, 95–210, 667–777; Fourteenth Congress, First Session, 182–88, 214–27; Eighteenth Congress, First Session, 32–33, 167–204, 354–418, 1068–84. Also Moore, *Congressional Quarterly's Guide to U.S. Elections,* 254–55; Ames, *Proposed Amendments,* 80–84.

[26]Moore, *Congressional Quarterly's Guide to U.S. Elections,* 254–55.

[27]Senate, Fourteenth Congress, First Session, March 20, 1816, in *Annals of Congress,* 214. See also Senate, Twenty-Seventh Congress, Second Session, June 2, 1842, in *Congressional Globe,* 11 (June 6, 1842), 566.

[28]Moore, *Congressional Quarterly's Guide to U.S. Elections,* 255.

Dividing the House

The split based on state size resurfaced in yet another arena: the decennial conflicts over reapportioning the House of Representatives. The first, and in many ways paradigmatic, controversy over apportionment occurred during the second Congress, in 1791–92, after the results of the first census had been reported. Although the Constitution had specified that representation in the lower house should be based on population, with not more than one representative for every thirty thousand people, it left up to Congress the determination of the total number of representatives, the precise ratio of people to representatives, and the division of representatives among the individual states.[29]

As Congress began debating the issue in November 1791, legislators began to realize the complexity of the task they faced. In addition to establishing a ratio between representatives and constituents, Congress had to determine whether it would fix the number of seats in the House, then divide the total population by that number to arrive at the ratio, or set the ratio and divide the total population by it to arrive at the number of seats; whether the number of representatives a state received should be based on the country's aggregate population or on the state's individual populations; and whether states should receive additional representation for so-called fractional remainders. Each of these variables affected the number of representatives a state—or group of states— would receive.

Almost immediately, a clash developed between a group of states calling themselves large and another group identifying themselves as small. Historian Rudolf M. Bell has done a roll-call analysis of eighteen crucial votes on apportionment in the second House of Representatives. Although each representative voted separately, delegates from the same state tended to vote with other members from their state on apportionment issues. Bell concluded, "Two separate groups emerged, each more than 90-percent cohesive in upholding its position."[30] One group consisted of New York, Pennsylvania, Maryland, Virginia, North Carolina, South Carolina, and Georgia—a coalition of large states, in other words. On the other side were Rhode Island, Connecticut, Massachusetts, New Hampshire, New Jersey, and Vermont—many of the

[29]Edmund J. James, "The First Apportionment of Federal Representatives in the United States," *Annals of the American Academy of Political and Social Science*, 9 (1897), 1–41; Rudolf M. Bell, *Party and Faction in American Politics: The House of Representatives, 1789– 1801* (Westport, Conn., 1973), 40–44; Michael L. Balinski and H. Peyton Young, *Fair Representation: Meeting the Ideal of One Man, One Vote* (New Haven, Conn., 1982), 5–22.
[30]Bell, *Party and Faction*, 41.

familiar small states.[31] Delaware did not vote consistently enough to be allied with any group.[32]

Bell does not call the former group the large states and the latter the small states, but people at the time did. Although the two groups were not identical to the large- and small-state coalitions at the Constitutional Convention, an evident continuity existed.[33] Pennsylvania, Virginia, North Carolina, South Carolina, and Georgia had all been members of the large-state bloc at the federal Convention. New York had always been an anomaly in the small-state alliance and now switched to the large-state coalition. By the 1790 census Maryland had grown to the sixth largest state in population and, not coincidentally, had begun to vote as a member of the large-state alliance. Among the small states, Connecticut and New Jersey had been members of the small-state alliance at the federal Convention. Rhode Island, New Hampshire, and Vermont had not participated in the representation debates at the Convention but were small states in every sense of the term. Only Massachusetts moved from the large-state to the small-state bloc, perhaps in anticipation of losing the district of Maine. (See appendix 4.)

Representatives from the self-proclaimed large and small states disagreed on almost every major aspect of apportionment. The question of the lower house's size created immediate dissension between the two groups. The large states urged that the House of Representatives be increased from 105 to 120 members; the small states supported the smaller number. A few years earlier, when discussing a similar proposal, Representative John Lawrence of New York had described why this issue would continue to divide the states:

> New Hampshire, Rhode Island, Connecticut, Jersey, and Delaware, would ever oppose an augmentation of the number of representatives; because their influence in the House would be proportionably abated. These States were incapable of extending their population beyond a certain point, inasmuch as they were confined with respect to territory. If, therefore, they could never have more than one representative, they would hardly consent to double that of the others, by which their own importance would be diminished.[34]

The larger the House, the smaller the small states' influence would be, because these states would never have more than a few representa-

[31]Ibid., 276n.24, 203–7.
[32]Ibid., 42, table 13.
[33]See chapter 3 for the alliances at the federal Convention.
[34]House of Representatives, First Congress, First Session, August 14, 1789, in *Annals of Congress*, 754.

tives—so they continually advocated a smaller House. The Senate, where the small states had more power, initially voted for 105 members, whereas the House, in which the larger states had more influence, supported a compromise measure providing for 112 members.[35]

Large- and small-state representatives also clashed over the proper ratio of people to representatives. The larger states desired the ratio of 30,000 to 1 set forth in the House bill; the small-state representatives supported the Senate's proposal of 33,000 to 1. Pure expediency dictated the states' stands on this issue. Congressmen on both sides figured out a number that would go most evenly into their state's population. The number 30,000 was found to go more evenly into the populations of the larger states. In other words, there was a smaller fractional remainder—a smaller unrepresented population—in the larger states than in the small when the divisor was 30,000. A divisor of 33,000 favored the smaller states. James Hillhouse of Connecticut remarked, "This ratio of thirty thousand throws an additional weight of seven Representatives into the scale of the large States."[36] Virginia, in particular, would receive 21 seats when its fair share was only 19.531. Representative Fisher Ames of Massachusetts noted that although the small states of Vermont, New Hampshire, Rhode Island, Connecticut, New Jersey, and Delaware possessed over 130,000 more people than Virginia, those states together would receive no more members than that single state alone.[37] Skillful arithmetic manipulation of the divisors could make a big difference in representation.

Another controversial subject dividing the large and small states concerned what to do with the fractional remainders. No number existed that would divide evenly into the populations of all the states. For example, if a state had a population of 100,000 and the ratio of people to representatives was 30,000 to 1, then the state would receive three representatives. But what would happen to the remaining 10,000 people? Either they would not be officially represented or the real ratio of people to representatives would be 33,333 to 1. Both cases presented potential problems. If Congress wanted to give additional representatives to states with fractional remainders, it had to decide on what basis to assign these extra delegates. Some representatives, influenced by Treasury Secretary Alexander Hamilton, urged that the states be ranked according to the size of their fractional remainders. Those states having

[35]Balinski and Young, *Fair Representation*, 10–22.

[36]Senate, Second Congress, First Session, December 19, 1791, in *Annals of Congress*, 259–62, 265; Balinski and Young, *Fair Representation*, 14–15.

[37]Senate, Second Congress, First Session, December 19, 1791, in *Annals of Congress*, 255.

the largest remainders would receive an additional representative, until all the remaining representatives had been distributed.[38]

Small-state delegates objected to this proposal. They argued that it was not the absolute size of the remainder but the percentage of the state's unrepresented population that mattered most. In the smaller states, fractional remainders composed a larger proportion of the state's total population. Because the smaller states were losing the most, they should be the first to receive additional representatives. "There was a great difference," said Elias Boudinot of New Jersey, "between the surplus of a smaller State represented by a single member, and that of a larger one, whose representation is more numerous; as the wants, the wishes, and the intentions of the constituents, are better represented in the latter case than the former."[39]

James Madison, however, refuted the point: "Gentlemen seemed to think," he said, "that the larger States would not suffer so much from those inequities as the smaller ones." He asked whether "the people in every part of the United States were not to be considered as equal on the floor of Congress? Ten or twenty thousand citizens of New York, North Carolina, or Virginia, when considered in relation to that House were of as much consequence as the same number in Rhode Island or Delaware."[40] Madison and other large-state delegates insisted that it was the absolute number of people left unrepresented that was the most important factor in granting additional representation. Thus the procedure benefiting the small states was thought to hurt the interests of the large.

Given their comments during the debates, it is also clear that many representatives saw the disputes of 1791–92 as a continuation of the conflict that had emerged at the federal Convention. Small-state representatives maintained that they had made a major concession by relinquishing the equal vote in Congress. They continued to insist that the small states had a set of interests distinct from that of the large states. During a discussion of House size, Jonathan Dayton of New Jersey asserted, "The great States would thus combine their influence, whenever they should deem it for their advantage, and . . . the interests of the other States would of consequence become the sacrifice."[41] Elbridge Gerry of Massachusetts, however, reiterated the disbelief that large-state delegates had expressed at the Convention. "The gentleman

[38]Balinski and Young, *Fair Representation*, 15–16.

[39]House of Representatives, Second Congress, First Session, January 24, 1792, in *Annals of Congress*, 335.

[40]Ibid., 334.

[41]House of Representatives, Second Congress, First Session, November 21, 1791, in *Annals of Congress*, 202.

had talked of combinations in the larger States," he said, "but . . . no facts could be produced to support such an apprehension."[42]

Certain large-state members believed that the apportionment issue gave them an opportunity to redress their grievances against the small states. Resenting the compromise they had been forced to make at the federal Convention, they believed that representation in both houses should be based on population. The equal vote in the Senate, they claimed, gave the small states a share of power not warranted by their populations. In justifying the number 30,000 as a divisor, for example, some large-state representatives said that any resulting unfairness to the small states was permissible to redress the injustice done at the Convention.[43] But other delegates attacked this reasoning. Theodore Sedgwick of Massachusetts (whose state voted with the small states on this particular issue) argued:

> Gentlemen had seemed to wish to obscure the merits of the present controversy, by considering it as a contest between the larger and smaller States, and by supposing that the latter would be compensated for their loss of weight and influence in this House, which would result from an unequal apportionment of representation, by the undue influence which they possessed in the Senate. . . . Justice, however, obliged him to declare that this mode of conducting the argument, only tended to divert the judgment from the true merits of the question.[44]

Fisher Ames, also of Massachusetts, was even more blunt: "Because the great States suffer wrong in the constitutional compact, will this bill do them right?"[45] The answer, according to the large-state members, was a qualified yes.

Like the controversy at the federal Convention, the apportionment controversy of 1791–92 ended in compromise—although the large states apparently received the better end of the deal. On March 23, 1792, the two houses finally agreed on an apportionment bill that increased the House's size to 120 members and distributed the representatives among the states. Although no explicit divisor was stated, it was assumed that there would be one representative for every thirty thousand people in the country as a whole, not according to each state's individual population. The states with the largest fractional remainders received addi-

---

[42]Ibid., 203.

[43]See, for example, House of Representatives, Second Congress, First Session, December 12, 1791, in *Annals of Congress*, 243–47.

[44]House of Representatives, Second Congress, First Session, December 19, 1791, in *Annals of Congress*, 271.

[45]Ibid., 257.

tional representatives.[46] The bill was sent to President George Washington, who unexpectedly vetoed it. Congress quickly passed another bill, which met his rather technical objections.[47]

State size was but one of many divisions that prolonged the apportionment debates of 1791–92. Supporters of northern and southern interests staked out positions, and supporters of Hamilton and of Jefferson also made their proposals clear. But the division between the large and small states was, in many ways, the most critical. At this time, the small states composed almost half of the Union and thus exercised a significant influence in the Senate. The large states dominated the House, where population determined representation. Only when differences between these two coalitions were resolved could any bill be passed. The passage of the 1792 apportionment act thus depended on a compromise between the large- and small-state alliances, which facilitated approval by both houses.

Compromise, however, was not capitulation. Neither side was prepared to give up the struggle. The decennial reapportionment came to be a forum for the resurgence of conflict between the large and small states. With slight variations, the scene enacted in 1791–92 was replayed once a decade until 1850.[48] Congress usually determined the number and distribution of representatives by arriving at a figure that maximized the representation in enough states to enable the bill to pass. But the large states called the shots, and only those small states that happened to benefit voted for the measures. A congressman surveying the history of reapportionment commented in 1850, "The work has been usually accomplished by a combination of the large States, who could best afford to bear the loss of the fractions, hitting upon some ratio that would leave them with small fractions, and then, with the aid of such small States as happened to have small fractions also under the proposed ratio, voting it through without much regard to the number of the House, and to the

[46]House of Representatives, Second Congress, First Session, March 23, 1792, in *Annals of Congress*, 482–83.

[47]Senate, Second Congress, First Session, April 9, 1792, in *Annals of Congress*, 119, 120; Balinski and Young, *Fair Representation*, 16–17, 20–21. Washington rejected the bill, on the advice of Thomas Jefferson, for two reasons: first because, he said, the bill did not enumerate a single divisor that, when applied to the states, produced the stated number of representatives; and second because, he maintained, the Constitution prescribed that the ratio of representatives to people could not exceed 1 to 30,000, as applied to the population of each state, not to the country's aggregate population, as the bill stated.

[48]*Annals of Congress:* Seventh Congress, First Session, 42–46, 333–42, 365–404; Eleventh Congress, Third Session, 402–31; Twelfth Congress, First Session, 402–13; Seventeenth Congress, First Session, 734–43, 806–24, 854–66, 881–910; Twenty-Second Congress, First Session, 502–30, 834–66. Also Twenty-Seventh Congress, Second Session, in *Congressional Globe*, 11 (April 28, 1842), 435–46; 11 (May 28, 1842), 532–34.

injustice done to the small States."[49] The large states, then, essentially dictated the terms of reapportionment to the small states. Furthermore, there was no single formula at work, just simple expediency.

The Impending Conflict

Over the years, the conflict based on size became intertwined with sectionalism. The more broadly based tension between North and South began to permeate disputes that had been based primarily on size. A glimpse of this tendency appeared in the districting debate of 1842. Several legislators commented that the movement toward the general-ticket system in electing congressmen would benefit the North and hurt the South. As Representative Campbell of South Carolina pointed out, "On all the questions peculiar to Southern interests, the Northern States, owing to the district system, were now divided, while the Southern voted in solid phalanx; but let the general ticket system prevail, and they would overwhelm the South."[50] Southerners, then, had a stake in promoting the district system or, at the very least, in stopping the spread of at-large elections. Representative Edward Everett of Massachusetts saw the issue in even more dire terms. He considered the district plan, he said, "as essential to the peace and well-being of the Union. . . . What was, in fact, our safety now? Only this: that the States were so divided in opinion, that the portions were balanced against each other, and neutralized each other's strength."[51] The adoption of district elections for congressmen was portrayed as a means of mitigating sectional conflict as well as benefiting the small states.

Sectionalism also affected apportionment. Although sectional tensions had always played a role in the debates over apportionment, by the mid-nineteenth century the situation was worsening. During the 1842 debate, southerners charged that the proposed distribution of representatives was unfair to them.[52] Soon afterward, divisive sectional issues such as the Wilmot Proviso, the Mexican War, and the proposed admission of

[49]House of Representatives, Thirty-First Congress, First Session, April 30, 1850, in *Congressional Globe*, 21 (May 1, 1850), 863.

[50]House of Representatives, Twenty-Seventh Congress, Second Session, April 26, 1842, in *Congressional Globe*, 11 (April 28, 1842), 445; Shields, "Whigs Reform the 'Bear Garden,'" 371.

[51]House of Representatives, Twenty-Seventh Congress, Second Session, May 2, 1842, in *Congressional Globe*, 11 (May 2, 1842), 464.

[52]Senate, Twenty-Seventh Congress, Second Session, May 24, 1842, in *Congressional Globe*, 11 (May 25, 1842), 526–27.

Texas to the Union came to the fore. Federal representatives spent much of 1850 hammering out a compromise that would ease these tensions.

In that same year, congressmen looked ahead to the next apportionment with trepidation, realizing that it might undo all the good accomplished by the Compromise. Congressman David Kaufman of Texas warned:

> Formerly the struggle [over apportionment] was mainly between the larger and the smaller States, but the indications arising from the feeling now existing in the country clearly showed that it would be converted into a sectional question; and if the North should undertake to trespass or encroach upon the rights of the South, to one hair's breadth, a storm, such an excitement of feeling, would be created throughout this country as had never before occurred during the existence of this Government.[53]

Seeking to forestall such a dispute, Representative Samuel F. Vinton of Ohio proposed that Congress adopt a permanent reapportionment act— even before the census results were reported. He argued that the framers of the Constitution had intended for there to be only one method of dividing representatives, not a "disreputable scramble to throw the fractions from one State or section upon another" every ten years.[54] He presented a formula for distributing representatives that first fixed the size of the House and then divided the seats. The country's aggregate population was divided by the chosen number of congressmen, and this quotient became the ratio of people to representatives.[55]

Congress saw the wisdom of the measure and approved it in 1850. Rather than discussing reapportionment every ten years and allowing simple expediency to prevail, Congress now had a rational plan for distributing representatives to the states. "Vinton's Method of 1850," as it became known, established the procedure that would last well into the twentieth century.[56] The remaining arena of conflict between the large and small states had thus been eradicated. Fear of increased sectional antagonism had led to an abolition of the basis of conflict between large and small states. In the end, the controversy based on state size had merged with, and become subsumed by, the sectional conflict.

[53]House of Representatives, Thirty-First Congress, First Session, May 7, 1850, in *Congressional Globe*, 21 (May 7, 1850), 927.

[54]House of Representatives, Thirty-First Congress, First Session, April 30, 1850, in *Congressional Globe*, 21 (May 1, 1850), 863.

[55]Moore, *Congressional Quarterly's Guide to U.S. Elections*, 686; Balinski and Young, *Fair Representation*, 37.

[56]Moore, *Congressional Quarterly's Guide to U.S. Elections*, 686.

The End of the Politics of Size

From 1776 to 1850, states identified themselves as members of the large- or small-state coalitions and, on representation questions, voted accordingly. Yet, as new states were added and old states gained or lost population, the precise configurations of the alliances changed. Among the original thirteen states, however, a core group emerged on each side. The members of each group consistently supported only one coalition, deviating no more than once from other members of their faction on representation votes. In the six major representation votes examined in appendix 4, the core members of the small-state alliance were Rhode Island, Connecticut, New Jersey, and Delaware. The mainstays of the large-state bloc were Massachusetts, New York, Pennsylvania, Virginia, North Carolina, South Carolina, and Georgia. Only two states, New Hampshire and Maryland, did not vote consistently enough with either faction to be firmly identified with one or the other—perhaps because of rapid changes in their populations. (See appendix 4.) Even beyond the original states, however, the rhetoric of state size continued to be invoked in representation debates and continued to have meaning for participants.

As in earlier conflicts over representation, the large- and small-state coalitions approached the issues of congressional districting, apportionment, and the selection of presidential electors from radically divergent points of view. Because both sides continued to assume that a state's size determined the extent of its potential population growth, each continued to see a fundamental conflict of interest between the two groups. Their limited growth prospects led the small states to insist on the primacy of communities, or territorial units, in representation questions. It also led them to stress the sacrifice they had made by relinquishing the equal vote at the federal Convention—a sacrifice that now left them, they argued, in a vulnerable position. Senator Dayton of New Jersey asserted in 1803: "The large states would threaten us with their power. The same threats had been heard in the old Congress, . . . [and] in the convention. . . . The gentleman had talked of a classification of States as a novelty, but [I] would ask that gentleman if he pretended to be wiser than the Constitution? Look through that instrument from beginning to end, and you will not find an article which is not founded on the presumption of a clashing of interests."[57]

Small-state representatives attempted to mitigate the negative effects

[57]Senate, Eighth Congress, First Session, November 24, 1803, in *Annals of Congress*, 100–101.

of the constitutional Compromise by holding at-large elections for congressmen and presidential electors—a tactic that gave them strength disproportionate to their populations—and by vetoing laws contrary to their interests when they came before the Senate. The small states, then, accepted the Union on their own terms, without fully accepting the principles of demographic representation. Only when self-interest led them to defect from the small-state alliance or their numbers became so small that they could no longer defend their interests did they abandon their chosen conception.

In contrast, the greater prospects for growth and the mobility of their populations led representatives from the large states to see representation in terms of randomly associated individuals rather than communities, in terms of population rather than territory. The superiority of the large states in numbers and area entitled them, they believed, to greater power than that of their smaller neighbors. Senator Wilson Nicholas of Virginia explained in 1803: "Extent of territory, occupied by a numerous population, is in a State, what wealth is to the private individual. The State of small extent, or of comparatively small population, stands in the same relation to society as the poor man. . . . The wealthy have, besides their civil rights, their property at stake, and may therefore be supposed more vigilant and watchful of innovations which may weaken or destroy that security by which they hold their rights and privileges."[58]

The large states felt cheated by the constitutional Compromise that gave the small states an equal vote in the Senate and angered by the small states' attempts to gain disproportionate power through at-large elections of congressmen and presidential electors. They believed that the system perpetuated a basic injustice against them—and sought to eliminate it. In the end, they were largely successful. Their notion of representation, in which population was the most important variable, prevailed over the small states' spatial conception.

Given the nature of the conflicting interests between large and small states, it is not at all surprising that the split emerged only in a very particular context: during discussions of representation questions. Yet the limited dimensions of the conflict do not in any way diminish the significance of the division. Participants on both sides realized that the resolution of structural and procedural matters, such as apportionment and the election of congressmen and presidential electors, would decide the very distribution of power among the states. They provided the basis for all other decisions and therefore were among the most important decisions Congress could make. The persistence of the controversy be-

[58]Ibid., 104.

tween large and small states reflected the depth of these concerns. On representation questions, size did materially affect a state's interests.

Although never as significant as the split between North and South, the division based on state size had important effects on congressional politics. Indeed, the very existence of the cleavage may have played a crucial role in preventing sectional lines from hardening within the national legislature. Coalitions based on state size cut across other divisions, uniting representatives from the North with those from the South. As long as size remained a basis for coalition-building, Virginians, North Carolinians, South Carolinians, and Georgians found themselves on the same side as delegates from Massachusetts, New York, and Pennsylvania on votes concerning representation. (See appendix 4.) Because the alliances based on size transcended sections, they reminded representatives from all regions of the continuing possibility for cooperation and compromise.

It is probably no accident that after the forcible eradication of the division based on state size in 1850, the antagonism between North and South deepened. Within Congress, alliances came to be based primarily, if not exclusively, on geography. Both sides grew more intractable and unwilling to reconcile their differences. Although the end of the large- and small-state controversy did not lead the country directly into civil war, it contributed to the increasing stalemate between sections. In the end, the abolition of the split based on state size cleared the way for an even more divisive confrontation between North and South.

EPILOGUE

Beyond Boundlessness

After liberating themselves from English rule, Americans became pre-occupied with the territory they had inherited from Great Britain—its extent, topography, population, and natural resources. Asserting their newfound nationalism, American writers declared that it was time for Americans to write their own geographies. "Europeans have been the sole writers of American Geography," noted Jedidiah Morse in his *American Universal Geography* of 1796, "and have too often suffered fancy to supply the place of facts, and thus have led their readers into errors."[1] Distinguished figures such as Thomas Jefferson, David Ramsay, Jeremy Belknap, and Hugh Williamson produced numerous works detailing the characteristics of the states and the nation. One geographer even suggested that the country's old name was inappropriate and that the nation should be renamed. "The 'United States,'" wrote Horatio Gates Spafford in 1809, "is a mere political title, and . . . we want a geographical one."[2] He proposed that the country be called Fredon and its inhabitants Fredonians to celebrate the freedom the inhabitants enjoyed.

These geographers reflected Americans' growing acceptance of their

[1] Jedidiah Morse, *The American Universal Geography, or a View of the Present State of All the Empires, Kingdoms, States, and Republics in the Known World, and of the United States of America in Particular* (Boston, 1796), preface.

[2] Horatio Gates Spafford, *General Geography and Rudiments of Useful Knowledge* (Hudson, N.Y., 1809), 129, 151–52. See also David Ramsay, *The History of South-Carolina* (Charleston, S.C., 1809); Thomas Jefferson, *Notes on the State of Virginia*, ed. Thomas Perkins Abernethy (New York, 1964; orig. publ. 1785); Jeremy Belknap, *The History of New-Hampshire* (Boston, 1792); Hugh Williamson, *The History of North-Carolina* (Philadelphia, 1812).

country's extensive size. Rather than bemoan the nation's large size, citizens began to come to terms with, even embrace, the vast expanses. "The extensive boundaries of the United States," said Joseph Scott in his *Gazetteer* of 1795, "the rapid increase of population, commerce and wealth, which has taken place in consequence of our happy revolution, the establishment of numerous towns, and settlements . . . render it impossible for every individual to obtain a personal knowledge of the whole."[3] Knowing that they could not personally acquaint themselves with all parts of their nation, Americans turned to maps and to the science of geography to familiarize themselves with their surroundings. Brimming with facts, figures, and vivid descriptions, the geographies and natural histories bridged the distances between Americans by providing factual information of all sorts.[4]

These geographies also reflected a growing sense that extensive territory was no longer a threat to republican government but a boon to its development. The nation's boundaries seemed elastic, capable of indefinite expansion. "In contemplating the vast field of the American empire," announced Gilbert Imlay in 1793, "what a stupendous subject does it afford for speculation! government, ethics, and commerce, acting upon principles different in many respects from those of the old world, and entirely [new] in others! A government which, with its spreading branches, seems in its mighty grasp to promise liberty and protection in one hemisphere!"[5] The nation's potential seemed virtually unlimited. A foreign visitor commented in 1820: "The fact is, that every sapient prophecy with regard to America has been disproved. We were forewarned that she was . . . too large, and her size has insured her union. These numerous republics, scattered through so wide a range of territory, embracing all the climates and containing the various products of the earth, seem destined, in the course of years, to form a world within themselves."[6] Long before the age of Manifest Destiny, many Americans had realized that extensive territory liberated rather than constrained them.

The change in Americans' perceptions of extensiveness resulted, at

---

[3]Joseph Scott, *The United States Gazetteer Containing an Authentic Description of the Several States* (Philadelphia, 1795), iii.

[4]The shift to a demographic notion of political representation coincided with and reflected the emergence of a statistical mentality in the United States. See Patricia Cline Cohen, *A Calculating People: The Spread of Numeracy in Early America* (Chicago, 1982), esp. 150–57; James H. Cassedy, *Demography in Early America: Beginnings of the Statistical Mind, 1600–1800* (Cambridge, Mass., 1969), esp. 307.

[5]Gilbert Imlay, *A Topographical Description of the Western Territory of North America* (New York, 1793), I: 74.

[6]"Frances Wright to a Friend," February 1820, in *The Early Republic, 1789–1828*, ed. Noble E. Cunningham, Jr. (New York, 1968), 274.

least in part, from a shift in assumptions about the theory and practice of representation. Federalist supporters of the U.S. Constitution articulated the conceptual framework behind this shift. They argued that large size, far from being a detriment to republican government, actually provided added stability by preventing the formation of factious majorities. Even more importantly, as long as the representation was sound, as long as the kind and quality of representatives was high, physical size was irrelevant to the republic's success. In effect, the Federalists challenged existing spatial assumptions about representation and constructed an alternative that did not depend on distance, size, or territory for its effectiveness.

Yet, although the theoretical justification for an extensive republic had been formulated even before the Constitution's ratification, it took a much longer time for practice to catch up. The residents of states with limited territory and relatively small populations continued to think about representation in spatial terms. They presumed that geography represented the most fundamental variable in constructing representative institutions. As a result, they located their new capitals according to geographic considerations, retained corporate apportionment in their legislatures, advocated the equal representation of state communities at the federal Convention, and worked to perpetuate the representation of the states through at-large elections of congressmen and presidential electors.

The citizens of states having enormous unsettled regions and a large, heterogeneous, geographically mobile population faced a very different set of problems and issues. They began to think demographically about representation questions, choosing to locate new state capitals at demographic centers, adopting proportional representation in the lower houses of their legislatures, advocating proportional representation in Congress, and supporting district elections for congressmen and presidential electors. Their situation forced them to realize that population, not territory, was the most important variable in structuring their institutions of representative government.

The small states' understanding of representation, which included but was not limited to territorial apportionment, can be called spatial representation. The large states' understanding of representation, which included but was not limited to numerical apportionment, can be called demographic representation.

Demographic representation revolutionized American political representation forever. Representation systems did—and do—inherently possess a spatial component. Some geographic unit is always going to be considered in establishing the basis of representation. What Americans did, however, was introduce population into calculations about representation and make it the most fundamental factor in establishing representative institutions. They changed the basis of representation from territory to population. Geographic boundaries, they showed, were malleable, subject to change as the population changed. They introduced the concept of the district—"a new species of political society," as William Pitt Beers of Connecticut called it[7]—whose boundaries could be redrawn as necessary. The individual replaced the community as the basic unit of apportionment. Legislators, Americans insisted, represented a certain number of people, not a cohesive community. Equal numbers of people, they argued, deserved equal numbers of representatives. As axiomatic as these principles seem today, they were not always so. In fact, it took an extended struggle between the large and small states to establish the demographic ideal.

By the mid-nineteenth century, demographic representation had acquired a virtual hegemony throughout the United States. The Federalists, victors in the struggle over the Constitution, had after all sanctioned the view. Moreover, states having the most territory and the majority of people had accepted it. Over time, more states—old and new alike—came to adopt proportional representation in their legislatures, leaving those that retained corporate representation in a dwindling minority.[8] In 1842, Congress moved to impose demographic representation in congressional elections, requiring states to elect their federal representatives by the district method alone. In 1850, Congress took a further step toward demographic representation by ending the decennial conflict between large and small states over apportionment in the lower house. It was not surprising, then, that many citizens began to believe that spatial representation was not only inequitable but also unrepublican. As Joseph Alston of South Carolina put it, "The most correct, the most republican system, is that of representation according to population."[9]

Despite some reversion to inequitable representation patterns in the late nineteenth and twentieth centuries,[10] demographic representation in all its forms had come to be identified with American government. By

[7]William Pitt Beers, *An Address to the Legislature and People of the State of Connecticut, on the Subject of Dividing the State into Districts for the Election of Representatives in Congress* (New Haven, Conn., 1791), 12.

[8]Malcolm E. Jewell and Samuel C. Patterson, *The Legislative Process in the United States* (New York, 1966), 50; Wilder Crane, Jr., and Meredith W. Watts, Jr., *State Legislative Systems* (Englewood Cliffs, N.J., 1968), 24–25; Gordon E. Baker, *The Reapportionment Revolution: Representation, Political Power, and the Supreme Court* (New York, 1966), 16–21.

[9]Joseph Alston, *Speech of Joseph Alston, Member of the House of Representatives for Winyaw, in a Committee of the Whole* . . . (Georgetown, S.C., 1808), 5.

[10]Jewell and Patterson, *Legislative Process*, 48–49; Baker, *Reapportionment Revolution*, 21–31; Crane and Watts, *State Legislative Systems*, 25.

the mid-twentieth century, any other alternative had become unthinkable. As Chief Justice Earl Warren wrote in the 1964 Supreme Court decision on *Reynolds v. Sims*, "Legislators represent people, not trees or acres."[11] Or as Justice William Brennan wrote in a 1983 New Jersey apportionment decision, "Adopting any standard other than population equality, using the best census data available, would subtly erode the Constitution's ideal of equal representation."[12]

Proportional representation may indeed be more equitable than the alternatives, but it is historically inaccurate to ascribe this "ideal" to the nation's founders. The Constitution embodied the principles of both corporate and proportional apportionment, spatial and demographic representation. Furthermore, no consensus existed among the framers, or the state governments, as to which method was the most republican.[13] Only the subsequent triumph of the demographic approach—secured through the large states' efforts—makes it unquestionable today.

Without the limitations imposed by spatial representation, nothing seemed to constrain American expansion. Historian Drew McCoy has argued that Americans wanted to expand across space to avoid the ravages of time, to escape the corruption and degeneration that had been endemic to republics. By spreading across the continent, Americans would have access to the virgin land that would ensure a virtuous, industrious citizenry.[14] This sense of infinite possibility gave antebellum America what John Higham calls "a spirit of boundlessness."[15] The American continent seemed to exist merely to provide an outlet for the nation's territorial ambitions.

[11]Stanley L. Kutler, ed., *The Supreme Court and the Constitution: Readings in American Constitutional History*, 2d ed. (New York, 1977), 596.

[12]Linda Greenhouse, "High Court Voids Jersey Districting for Seats in House," *New York Times*, June 23, 1983, A1, B10.

[13]I do not mean to suggest that the framers' intent should be the primary basis for judging the constitutionality of apportionment schemes; rather, I mean to emphasize the lack of historical accuracy in such pronouncements. Justice Felix Frankfurter made a similar point in his dissent from the majority decision in *Baker v. Carr:* "The notion that representation proportioned to the geographic spread of population is so universally accepted as a necessary element of equality between man and man that it must be taken to be the standard of a political equality preserved by the Fourteenth Amendment . . . is, to put it bluntly, not true. However desirable and however desired by some among the great political thinkers and framers of our government, it has never been generally practiced, today or in the past. It was not the English system, it was not the colonial system, it was not the system chosen for the national government by the Constitution, it was not the system exclusively or even predominantly practiced by the states at the time of the adoption of the Fourteenth Amendment, it is not predominantly practiced by the States today." Kutler, *Supreme Court*, 592.

[14]Drew McCoy, *The Elusive Republic: Political Economy in Jeffersonian America* (Chapel Hill, N.C., 1980), esp. 75–84, 196–203.

[15]John Higham, *From Boundlessness to Consolidation: The Transformation of American Culture, 1848–1860* (Ann Arbor, Mich., 1969), 6.

Boundlessness, however, contained within itself the seeds of its own destruction. By the mid-nineteenth century, state size had been eliminated as a significant division among states. In its place, however, sectionalism came to exert an even more divisive influence. Because Americans had resolved the theoretical and the institutional problems associated with extensive size, both North and South regarded territorial expansion not only as a possibility but as a right. Far from being a threat to the republic, growth seemed essential to preserving each section's particular economic system and way of life. No check existed to restrain the territorial ambitions of these competing communities. Whereas a fundamental difference in values may have been able to coexist in an extensive republic whose size was static, a collision became inevitable in one that was expanding. Americans had disproved the *philosophes* in the short run only to prove them nearly correct in the long run.

The Removal of State Capitals, 1776–1812

State	Date removal act passed	Old and new capitals
Delaware	May 12, 1777	Newcastle to Dover
Virginia	June 12, 1779	Williamsburg to Richmond
Georgia	January 26, 1786	Savannah to Louisville (interim capital at Augusta until 1795)
	December 12, 1804	Louisville to Milledgeville
South Carolina	March 22, 1786	Charles Town to Columbia
North Carolina	August 4, 1788	New Bern and others to Raleigh
New Jersey	November 25, 1790	Burlington, Perth Amboy, and others to Trenton
New York	March 10, 1797	New York City and others to Albany
Pennsylvania	March 30, 1799	Philadelphia to Lancaster
	February 21, 1810	Lancaster to Harrisburg
New Hampshire	1808 (de facto)	Portsmouth and others to Concord
Rhode Island	Rotated*	Among Newport, Providence, East Greenwich, South Kingston, and Bristol
Connecticut	Rotated*	Between Hartford and New Haven

*"Rotated" means that the legislature's meetingplace was shifted between or among selected towns.

APPENDIX 2. Large- and Small-State Voting Patterns at the Federal Constitutional Convention

The following represent the most crucial votes on representation from the opening of the Convention until the passage of the Great Compromise:

Date	Vote	States	Vote	States	Divided	States
June 11[a]	*Aye*	Mass., Conn., Pa., Va., N.C., S.C., Ga.	*No*	N.Y., N.J., Del.	*Divided*	Md.
June 11[b]	*No*	Mass., Pa., Va., N.C., S.C., Ga.	*Aye*	Conn., N.Y., N.J., Del., Md.		
June 11[c]	*Aye*	Mass., Pa., Va., N.C., S.C., Ga.	*No*	Conn., N.Y., N.J., Del., Md.		
June 28–29[d]	*No*	Mass., Pa., Va., N.C., S.C., Ga.	*Aye*	Conn., N.Y., N.J., Del.	*Divided*	Md.
July 2[e]	*No*	Mass., Pa., Va., N.C., S.C.	*Aye*	Conn., N.Y., N.J., Del., Md.	*Divided*	Ga.
July 7[f]	*No*	Pa., Va., S.C.	*Aye*	Conn., N.Y., N.J., Del., Md., N.C.	*Divided*	Mass., Ga.
July 14[g]	*No*	Va., N.C., S.C., Ga., N.J.	*Aye*	Conn., —[i], Del., Md., Mass.	*Divided*	Pa.
July 16[h]	*No*	Pa., Va., S.C., Ga.	*Aye*	Conn., —[i], N.J., Del., Md., N.C.	*Divided*	Mass.

a"Resolved that the right of suffrage in the first branch of the national Legislature ought not to be according to the rule established in the articles of confederation; but according to some equitable ratio of representation." Max Farrand, ed., *The Records of the Federal Convention of 1787* (New Haven, Conn., 1911), I: 192–5. (Notes b–h are also from Farrand.)

b"That in the second branch of the National Legislature each State shall have One vote" (I: 192–95).

c"Resolved that the right of suffrage in the second branch of the national legislature ought to be according to the rule established for the first" (I: 192–95).

d"Resolved that the right of suffrage in the second branch of the Legislature of the United States ought to be according to the rule established in the articles of confederation" (I: 444, 460–61).

e"Resolved that in the second branch of the Legislature of the United States each State shall have an equal vote" (I: 509–10).

f"It was moved and seconded that the second proposition reported from the grand Committee stand part of the report namely 'That in the second branch of the Legislature each State shall have an equal vote'" (I: 548–49).

g"That to secure the liberties of the States already confederated, the number of representatives in the first branch, shall never exceed the representatives from such of the thirteen united states as shall accede to this Confederacy" (II: 1–2).

h"The question being taken on the whole of the report from the Grand Committee as amended" (II: 13, 15).

iNew York delegates left the Convention in mid-July.

APPENDIX 3

Party Distribution of Congressmen According to Method Of Election, 1789–1842

District		At-Large	
	FIRST CONGRESS (1789–1791)		
Massachusetts	2 Anti-administration	Connecticut	5 Pro-administration
	6 Pro-administration	Delaware	1 Pro-administration
New York	3 Anti-administration	New Hampshire	1 Anti-administration
	3 Pro-administration		2 Pro-administration
North Carolina	3 Anti-administration	New Jersey	4 Pro-administration
	2 Pro-administration	Pennsylvania	2 Anti-administration
South Carolina	3 Anti-administration		6 Pro-administration
	2 Pro-administration	Rhode Island	1 Pro-administration
Virginia	7 Anti-administration		
	3 Pro-administration		

Combination District/At-Large	
Georgia	3 Anti-administration
Maryland	4 Anti-administration
	2 Pro-administration

All information on party affiliation is derived from Kenneth Martis, *The Historical Atlas of Political Parties in the United States Congress, 1789–1987* (New York, forthcoming). (Information is based on initial elections.)

SIXTH CONGRESS (1799–1801)

Kentucky	2 Republicans	Connecticut	7 Federalists
Maryland	3 Republicans	Delaware	1 Federalist
	5 Federalists	Georgia	2 Federalists
Massachusetts	2 Republicans	New Hampshire	4 Federalists
	12 Federalists	Rhode Island	2 Federalists
New Jersey	3 Republicans		
	2 Federalists		
New York	6 Republicans		
	4 Federalists		
North Carolina	6 Republicans		
	4 Federalists		
Pennsylvania	8 Republicans		
	5 Federalists		
South Carolina	1 Republican		
	5 Federalists		
Tennessee	1 Republican		
Vermont	1 Republican		
	1 Federalist		
Virginia	13 Republicans		
	6 Federalists		

ELEVENTH CONGRESS (1809–1811)

Kentucky	6 Republicans	Connecticut	7 Federalists
Maryland	6 Republicans	Delaware	1 Federalist
	3 Federalists	Georgia	4 Republicans
Massachusetts	8 Republicans	New Hampshire	5 Federalists
	9 Federalists	New Jersey	6 Republicans
New York	10 Republicans	Ohio	1 Republican
	7 Federalists	Rhode Island	2 Federalists
North Carolina	9 Republicans		
	3 Federalists		
Pennsylvania	16 Republicans		
	2 Federalists		
South Carolina	8 Republicans		
Tennessee	3 Republicans		
Vermont	1 Republican		
	3 Federalists		
Virginia	17 Republicans		
	5 Federalists		

(*continued*)

SIXTEENTH CONGRESS (1819–1821)

Kentucky	10 Republicans	Alabama	1 Republican
Maryland	6 Republicans	Connecticut	7 Republicans
	3 Federalists	Delaware	1 Republican
Massachusetts	13 Republicans		1 Federalist
	7 Federalists	Georgia	6 Republicans
New York	22 Republicans	Illinois	1 Republican
	5 Federalists	Indiana	1 Republican
North Carolina	10 Republicans	Louisiana	1 Republican
	3 Federalists	Mississippi	1 Republican
Ohio	6 Republicans	New Hampshire	6 Republicans
Pennsylvania	19 Republicans	New Jersey	6 Republicans
	4 Federalists	Rhode Island	2 Republicans
South Carolina	9 Republicans	Vermont	6 Republicans
Tennessee	6 Republicans		
Virginia	20 Republicans		
	3 Federalists		

TWENTY-FIRST CONGRESS (1829–1831)

Alabama	3 Jacksonians	Connecticut	6 Anti-Jacksonians
Indiana	1 Jacksonian	Delaware	1 Anti-Jacksonian
	2 Anti-Jacksonians	Georgia	7 Jacksonians
Kentucky	10 Jacksonians	Illinois	1 Jacksonian
	2 Anti-Jacksonians	Mississippi	1 Jacksonian
Louisiana	1 Jacksonian	Missouri	1 Jacksonian
	2 Anti-Jacksonians	New Hampshire	6 Jacksonians
Maine	4 Jacksonians	New Jersey	6 Anti-Jacksonians
	3 Anti-Jacksonians	Rhode Island	2 Anti-Jacksonians
Maryland	6 Jacksonians		
	3 Anti-Jacksonians		
Massachusetts	13 Anti-Jacksonians		
New York	19 Jacksonians		
	12 Anti-Jacksonians		
	3 Anti-Masonics		
North Carolina	10 Jacksonians		
	3 Anti-Jacksonians		
Ohio	8 Jacksonians		
	6 Anti-Jacksonians		
Pennsylvania	24 Jacksonians		
	1 Anti-Jacksonian		
	1 Anti-Masonic		
South Carolina	9 Jacksonians		
Tennessee	8 Jacksonians		
	1 Anti-Jacksonian		
Vermont	4 Anti-Jacksonians		
	1 Anti-Masonic		
Virginia	16 Jacksonians		
	6 Anti-Jacksonians		

TWENTY-SIXTH CONGRESS (1839–1841)

	District		At-Large
Alabama	3 Democrats	Arkansas	1 Democrat
	2 Whigs	Delaware	1 Democrat
Connecticut	6 Whigs	Georgia	9 Whigs
Illinois	2 Democrats	Michigan	1 Democrat
	1 Whig	Mississippi	2 Democrats
Indiana	5 Democrats	Missouri	2 Democrats
	2 Whigs	New Hampshire	5 Democrats
Kentucky	2 Democrats	New Jersey	5 Democrats
	11 Whigs		1 Whig
Louisiana	3 Whigs	Rhode Island	2 Whigs
Maine	6 Democrats		
	2 Whigs		
Maryland	5 Democrats		
	3 Whigs		
Massachusetts	2 Democrats		
	10 Whigs		
New York	19 Democrats		
	21 Whigs		
North Carolina	8 Democrats		
	5 Whigs		
Ohio	11 Democrats		
	8 Whigs		
Pennsylvania	17 Democrats		
	5 Whigs		
	6 Anti-Masonics		
South Carolina	8 Democrats		
	1 Whig		
Tennessee	6 Democrats		
	7 Whigs		
Vermont	2 Democrats		
	3 Whigs		
Virginia	12 Democrats		
	7 Whigs		
	2 Conservatives		

APPENDIX 4. Large- and Small-State Coalitions, 1776–1842
(How the Original Thirteen States Divided According to Size on Six Key Issues)

SMALL-STATE POSITIONS

	Removal of state capitals[b]	Apportionment in the states[c]	Federal convention[d]	1791–92 Congressional apportionment[e]	Congressional elections, 1812	Congressional elections, 1842
	Geographic	Corporate	Equal-vote	"Small"-state	At-large	At-large
New Jersey ⎫	X	X	X	X	X	X
Connecticut ⎪	X	X	X	X	X	
Delaware ⎬ CORE[a]	X	X	X	X	X	X
Rhode Island ⎪	X	X	(not present)	(no consistent vote)	X	X
Maryland ⎭	X	X	X	X		
New Hampshire			(not present)			
Georgia	(second removal)			X	X	X
Massachusetts	(no removal)	X		X	X	
North Carolina		X				
New York	X		X			
South Carolina		X				
Virginia	X	X				
Pennsylvania		X				

LARGE-STATE POSITIONS

	Removal of state capitals[b]	Apportionment in the states[c]	Federal convention[d]	1791–92 Congressional apportionment[e]	Congressional elections, 1812	Congressional elections, 1842
	Demographic	Proportional	Proportional	"Large"-state	District	District
Pennsylvania ⎫	(both removals)	X	X	X	X	X
Georgia ⎬ CORE[a]	(first removal)	X	X	X		X
North Carolina ⎭	X	X	X	X	X	X
New York	X	X		X	X	X
South Carolina		X	X	X	X	X
Virginia	X	X	X	X	X	X

158

Massachusetts	(no removals)	X	X			X	X
Maryland						X	X
New Hampshire	X	X	(not present)	X			X
Connecticut					X		
Delaware				(no consistent vote)			
New Jersey							
Rhode Island		(not present)					

[a] A state is considered part of the core if it deviated no more than once from a particular coalition. Failure to participate in a particular vote is not counted as a failure to vote with the bloc.

[b] Location of new state capitals as of 1812.

[c] Apportionment of lower houses of the state legislatures as of 1812.

[d] Based on votes taken on June 11, 1787, before the deterioration of the large-state coalition.

[e] Based on Rudolf M. Bell's roll-call analysis of eighteen crucial votes on apportionment taken in the Second Congress. See Bell's *Party and Faction in American Politics: The House of Representatives, 1789–1801* (Westport, Conn., 1973), 276n.24.

Index

Library of Congress Cataloging-in-Publication Data

Zagarri, Rosemarie, 1957–
    The politics of size.

    Includes index.
    1. Representative government and representation—United States—
History. 2. Federal government—United States—History. 3. State
governments—History. I. Title.
JK1071.Z34   1987   321.02′0973   87-47609
ISBN 0-8014-2019-9 (alk. paper)